Hidden Heritage
Discovering Ancient Essex

Terry Johnson

Hidden Heritage
Discovering Ancient Essex

©1996 Terry Johnson

ISBN 1 898307 70 9

ALL RIGHTS RESERVED

No part of this publication may be reproduced, stored in a retrieval system or transmitted in any form or by any means, electronic, mechanical, photocopying, scanning, recording or otherwise without the prior written permission of the author and the publisher.

Cover design & illustration by Daryth Bastin

Published by:

>Capall Bann Publishing
>Freshfields
>Chieveley
>Berks
>RG20 8TF

Contents

Foreword	3
Chapter One Mysteries beneath our feet	5
Prehistoric sites defined	15
Earthworks	15
Holy and beacon hills	17
Barrows and mounds	19
Holy wells	20
Mazes	21
Castles	22
Dene holes and groves	22
Stone circles and standing stones	23
Preaching crosses	28
Chapter Two Church paganism	29
Gargoyles and grotesques	33
Green men	36
Tongue pokers and mouth pullers	37
Dragons	39
Exhibitionists	41
Animals	43
Solar carvings	43
Paintings	44
Chapter Three Discovering ley lines	45
Sample Essex leys described	54
Chapter Four Essex site gazetteer	59
Bibliography	176
Index	179

Acknowledgements

This book has been compiled from many sources including literature such as Essex village guide books, articles by Dr E.A.Rudge of the defunct Essex Field Club, numerous church leaflets, editions of ASH magazine and old and new Ordnance Survey maps.

I would especially like to thank Dave Hobbs for assisting me on many fruitful field trips and for his *'stone spotting'* ability, and John Ruse for the enormous wad of his research literature which he so generously loaned me.

Thanks also to Ian Dawson and Dave Hunt of ASH magazine for essentially broadening my interests. Without them this book would not have been attempted.

I further acknowledge all those Essex folk who aided me in-situ during the years of scouring the county, especially Mr Blackwell.

Nearer to home I am grateful to Mike and Dot Batley, Barbara Broadway, Fred Curtiss, John Griffin, *'Jack by the Hedge'*, Richard Johnson, Alex Langstone, Nigel Pennick, Carole Young and finally my wife Jean for putting up with all the gargoyle photos at home.

Foreword

When tasked to describing the prehistoric works of man it is tempting to cover the whole of the country. This allows the inclusion of the more interesting and impressive venues, but precludes numerical perspective, and in so doing tends to paint a false picture of the bygone British landscape. This is because of the enormous profusion of ancient works left by our forbears that are given scant or no recognition.

A comprehensive national listing would mount to a huge impractical volume, so, with the object of compiling the essence of an intense coverage I chose a single county that would exemplify the whole. Because I live there Essex was selected. Fortunately Essex is also reminiscent of most Eastern and Home Counties, terrain wise, and, farther afield, by dint of the nature of its earth and stone remains.

Choosing a county not boasting constructions of Stonehenge and Avebury fame illustrates that Neolithic peoples exercised their skills more prolifically, and over a wider area, than we are generally led to believe. I hope to demonstrate that rural mystery and intrigue is not confined to monuments of great visual impact alone. A time worn mark-stone, unobtrusively buried in nettles by a church wall can tell us as much in some ways as can glamourous circles of the shires.

One object of this publication is to encourage the reader to seek out little known sites themselves - in Essex and elsewhere - that are unmapped and half forgotten. Such hunting can be as exciting as visiting a grand, tourist-laden attraction. And who knows, you may add a piece of information to the jig-saw that is our hidden heritage.

Chapter One

Mysteries beneath our feet

Whenever the tourist or more adventurous traveller ponders on ancient mysterious places, visions of say, the Gizah pyramids, the lost cities of the Mayan Indians or the Cretan palace of Knossos might well spring to mind. If thoughts stray closer to home then we might well plumb for Glastonbury or some romantic castle steeped in Arthurian legend. Very few would think of Essex. Who goes to Essex to view a prehistoric wonder? We prefer our objectives to be on the map, of striking impact, preferably in a nice climate with souvenir brimming visitor centres vending tri-coloured ice-cream and tickets for a circumnavigating camel ride.

As for informative glossy brochures, citizens of lands such as Greece or Babylon have bequeathed us the written word, be it glyph or alphabet. In Egypt, once the tri-lingual Rosetta stone was liberated from the sand the way was cleared to translating scripts on everything from a royal cartouche to the destination tag on a Nile bound pomegranate crate. But no such stone has turned up in Britain, let alone Essex. Nor is one considered to be likely to. Our Island's past remains a blank page is compared to sunnier climes. Our pre-Roman cultures did not encourage the application of quill to parchment. Britons, who thrived when Egypt was wallowing in her prolific, city-building Middle Kingdom period, have left us with but a few enigmatic, geometric scribings on a few standing stones.

The Celtic druids and bards fostered the policy of committing knowledge to the now irretrievable mode of the human memory. The Romans, Saxons and Danes subsequently took scant interest in the conquered land's past, and besides, by their day they would have had to have been archaeologists themselves to have gleaned much from extant ruins, long had they fallen into disuse by then.

Since then the eroding march of time in a harsh climate, and destructive religious purges have dealt a heavy blow to the legacy of our ancestors. Stone circles like Avebury, although a wonderful experience to visit, are but fragments of their former selves. Most circles actually lay barely definable buried in bracken and well off the nearest sheep track. Surviving barrows and earthworks are also mainly reduced to the status of exclusion from the itinerary of all but the most informed enthusiast.

Essex has slid even further down the slopes to oblivion than most of our fair isle counties thanks to its creeks and rivers that gave easy access to rude continental invaders. In the flat arable landscape where the subterranean strata is clay, many remaining stone pillars became prime targets for building material. However, the one time kingdom of the East Saxons can boast scores of remnants today. What is more, if usually small, stones, for instance, are not usually lost in a sea of hindering heather. Instead, Essex stones tend to grace quaint village greens. The quantity, and indeed sometimes the quality of the remains causes us to consider that Essex has as rich a history as abundant Wessex. Those prepared to seek out or simply drive up to them can discover many survivors of forgotten Bronze Age and Neolithic millenniums to give reign to the imagination, romance or research.

Moreover, we should not look to visual magnificence in singular finds. Some of the mysterious ambience is only perceived when sites are viewed in what could be called a holistic manner. Much may be revealed from their intregal geographic relationship and from seldom considered intrinsic properties. Theories expounded as to their function, singly or as a whole have yet to be proven or otherwise. The study of stone and earthwork is a relatively recent undertaking, room is left for the reader to become usefully emersed in it.

Even today the image of stone age man is often one of a bear skinned Neanderthal brute tramping about dragging his wife by the hair. With a bone stuck through his nose our illiterate cave man eked out a living by thumping woolly mammoths with a club and cooking the beast over his newly discovered fire. His favourite word was 'ugg' which he grunted when pondering why his square wheel didn't revolve.

A more refined version is accepted by the archaeological world - if not so only thirty years ago - but our hairy ancestor still only lives in a mud hut, or as a nomadic hunter-gatherer, in hide shelters. To keep track of when to plant his emmer wheat he erected rudimentary stone circles to induce astro-alignments. As an alternative, priests would hold ceremonies in them on Sundays.

Objections to this hypothesis may well be valid. For astronomical readings, vast stones are not necessary. Simple wood staves would suffice that could easily be replaced when worn. It is also argued that farmers, who would most benefit from these markers, would not need any elaborate structure. Nature is abound with signs and portents to indicate when to sow and reap. Valid weather-saws were used into this century, and agriculture did not appear to plunge into disarray on the demise of circles.

As to ceremony, surely such was carried out, but again, circles are well over-the-top in terms of return for human effort. Furthermore, their locations seldom appear to have been chosen with that in mind. They are not on prominent hill crests or dramatic places. There is no evidence, for example, of a circle on Glastonbury Tor, surely a prime target. Circles are invariably entrenched undramatically half way up mediocre slopes and in bleak, out of the way spots that would be inconvenient for the villagers they served. If astro-alignments were sought then why are there not more on the coast with uninterrupted access to the heavens?

Returning to the theory that circles possess more than meets the eye, we could do well to turn to the work of Professor Thom of Oxford University. In the 1950s and 60s this surveyor toured some 600 circles measuring with a precision never before deployed. His conclusions caused a radical re-assessment of Neolithic culture.

Over 950 circles survive in various conditions. It is not known how many have succumbed to destruction but twice that many is accepted as realistic. They're distributed throughout the British isles including Ireland and Brittany but excluding eastern England, although, controversially this may not once have been so. But it is not controversial to speculate that the building period spanned at least 2000 years up to about 1500 BC, when the culture mysteriously seemed to collapse.

Only around 65% of circles are actually round, the remainder are elliptical, egg shaped or of a compound derivative. The diameters range from about 30 feet to 1400 feet with any number of stones from 4 to 400 and weighing anything up to 50 tons. The Brize stone in Brittany is a record 340 tons. Professor Thom submitted that a common length of measure of 2.72 feet/ 0.829 Metres was used, which he dubbed the Megalithic Yard. Our cave man also knew the value of Pi long before Pythagoras did! Apart from being single rings, circles can be concentric and include centre stones, outliers, avenues and graded sizes complete with a multiplicity of combinations. Stones come in a different material such as sarsen, limestone or breccia with examples being transported many miles to the site. The Stonehenge bluestones were dragged over 200 miles from the Presceli mountains yet Salisbury plain is abundant with sarsen stone which apparently would not do.

Since Thom's meticulous surveys other more unconventional forms of attention have been applied to megalithic stones. Rod and pendulum dowsers and 'psychics' claim that some stones possess some kind of property that could be described as electro-magnetic. The revival of ley-line hunting also contrived to arouse a fresh and unprecedented interest in our forgotten heritage.

Investigators began to pay attention to the age old Chinese art of Feng Shui, where terrestrial energies are a central theme. It then seemed probable that some lonely old stone in the corner of an Essex field was taking on a new dimension.

Victorian colonialists in China found that local officials would be alarmed when informed that a road or railway was to be built. They would protest that it was impossible on account that it would cut off the dragon's limbs. They would decry the westerner's lack of respect for Feng Shui, politely bow and exit the room.

One governor of Macau would have none of this 'superstitious nonsense' and deliberately drove roads and erected buildings in places designed to most upset them! He was eventually waylaid in the countryside and beheaded! Chinese officialdom simply shrugged and declared it the inevitable revenge of Feng Shui!

Feng Shui literally means wind and water. It is the complex art and science of reading the landscape so that a grave or important building may be sited where it would gain the maximum benefit from the unseen 'breath of nature'. Even today in Hong Kong constructions such as banks are situated in accord with Feng Shui geomancy with all manner of subsequent subterfuge, move and countermove going on to ensure that a rival bank, for instance, gains no advantage over it. Feng Shui even accounts for the internal arrangement of furniture and pot plants.

A century ago geomancers were treated with deference for their literacy and ability to understand the powers of nature, thus were often carried about in a sedan chair. They ensured that cosmic forces influenced the population in terms of health and prosperity. The finite aspects of the art probably suffers from distortion and social influence but the basic principles are most intriguing.

The science is abound with flowery terms such as the white tiger, red bird, earth, wood and dragon paths, and has similarities with western occult terminology. But it appears to be rooted in a systematic study of the physics of universal energies that our science today is not aware of. The 3000 year old wisdom uses quaint labels so as to allow intangible forces to be more readily grasped by an uneducated populace. The Chinese hypothesis of creation and the cosmos is far removed from the more typical and romantic variant as found in the Greek and Babylonian mythos.

The creative principles of yin and yang are perhaps familiar to some in this country. The symbol is that black and white circle resembling two intertwining tear drops. When it permeates the earth the Chinese refer to it as ch'i. It's twin aspects flow independently along sinuous paths called Lung Mei or dragon paths. Generally speaking yin flows through low terrain and water, and yang through mountains. The art of a geomancer is to divine the earth with a special compass, that also involves such arts as numerology, astrology and astronomy, in search of spots where yin and yang lines cross in a harmonious balance.

The rate of collection and dispersion of ch'i is also important. Ch'i is also said to condense and evaporate, it can be blown away, fail to breath in a flat terrain or suffer too rapid a dispersion by straight features or fast rivers. Gross imbalance can cause a malign influence. Five secondary elements play a part as modifiers and an imbalanced form of noxious, stagnated ch'i is called sha.

Parallels to Feng Shui can be identified in the medical practice of acupuncture. This too is centred on ch'i energy flowing along mei lines called meridians. An imbalance in the body leads to illness which can be rectified by tapping into certain points on the mei lines so as to clear the blockage. This would be the equivalent of a build up of sha.

Tom Graves, in his book. *Needles of Stone*, suggests that standing stones, being as they are sunk into the ground, are functionally similar to acupuncture needles. He speculates that stone might serve to redress terrestrial blockages, or at least the two techniques are a means of manipulating energy flows. The Chinese and ancient Britons might have sought the same ends by different means. The Chinese physically altered the landscape to redress ch'i. In Britain we drove large stones into it instead.

If the Chinese did identify an energy called ch'i it is notable that the Celts refer to 'nwyvre' which appears to be one and the same. Modern occultism has its ether and the Indians speak of prana. Unconventional researchers in Europe seemed to have arrived at the same conclusions, too, using names such as ond and orgone.

Stones have become the focus of earth mysteries investigators today. Conclusions of dowsers are that some stones have energy spirals around them, which tend to change direction in accord to lunar phases. A simple experiment for non dowsers is to place your hands on a stone and relax. It may become apparent why some stones are called Twizzle Stone or the like, or are associated with turning around or dancing. An effect can be to throw you off the stone as if by a repelling magnet. Other stones actually feel as if they are rocking, tingling or pulsing. A simple magnetic compass can reveal hidden forces, too. Limestone especially is usually formed around a core of quartz crystal. This mineral is used in watches as it has piezo-electrical properties that release a current when under physical pressure. A stone expanding and contracting in the heat of the day would produce this result.

It must be said here that dowsing alone can be problematic being as it is not repeatable science but an art dependant on human ability and frailty. Short pendulum dowsing does appear to be a latent faculty of the mind. Groups of people dowsing the same site all too often end up with conflicting results. But, allowing for it's shortcomings, its a flexible and cheap detection method.

For a repeatable result we must turn to technical gadgetry, allowing for the fact that nobody has come up with a ch'i detector yet. Researchers have, however, applied substitutes despite knowing little of frequencies, emission points or time cycles.

The Dragon Project was set up in the late seventies by the staff of the *Ley Hunter* magazine with the object of analysing energies at prehistoric sites by combining technical and intuitive methods. The project is still on-going but conclusions so far, from this and parallel endeavours by others, is that stone circles do emit unknown magnetic anomalies. Magnetometers and guassmeters have shown that the magnetic intensity inside their focal circle; the Rollright Stones, was lower than on the outside. Stones also pulse magnetically and are subject to the sun rise, some displaying spirals of energy, frequently in seven bands that reverse direction every six days after the full and new moons. A well known infra-red photograph, since repeated, shows the King Stone at Rollright at sun up with a yet unexplained discharge glow around it's top.

Ultra sound detectors have also shown pulse patterns apparently controlled by solar and lunar influences. Geiger counters reveal radiation anomalies in stone circles and not in the peripheral landscape.

The above aside, I personally find it quite remarkable that the culture in question is so overlooked. At first glance this is perhaps understandable. Ancient works are seen as merely ceremonial or calendric, no temple or palace foundation has been unearthed, no criss-cross city street traces, no carved slabs spill forth dates, places or successions of monarchs. We find little trace of international trade via paved roads or tall sailed caravelles.

But does this really indicate no more than scattered tribes with little internal communication and a coincidental passion for rings of stone and earth, as is popularly believed. Surely the extant remains are enough to strongly hint that Britain's civilisation was in many ways equal to it's more famous foreign counterparts. The lack of the usual finds could simply mean that by and large we are dealing with a race who's mentality, religion and modus operandi was different to their neighbours.

Let us take a look at what we have; a sample area, say, the hills around Avebury. This circle alone consisted of some 500 stones of up to 50 tons each together with a hand dug chalk rubble bank of

200.000 tons. Within an area of five miles across we have three more circles, Windmill Hill causeway camp, the five area Silbury Hill, two huge long barrows and a score of tumuli and earthworks. At the other end of the scale the backwater of Essex has probably 200 sites of this period. If we project this scale nation wide we come up with possibly tens of thousands of effort demanding structures. This alone is thought provoking, never mind the possibility of alignments and site selection by means suggesting a complex knowledge of terrestrial energies. All in all we have an area equal to most lands of pre-Roman times. To provide the manpower to construct it's circles, henges, causeway camps, fogue chambers, cairns, passage graves, tumuli and long barrows it must have had a population equal to any foreign shore. Technically it's legacy reveals an understanding of mathematics, astronomy and geometry to rival the Mayans and Egyptians.

Furthermore, to survive 200 years this society must have been very stable with a strong government and a unified nation incentive. As well as it's task of supplying the people's everyday needs it had to cope with a huge building project with its demand of food land material logistics, authoritative control, communication and transportation.

The British Isles has no smooth convenient Nile or balmy seas between idyllic islands, her peoples had to deal with dense forests, rugged mountains, rough seas and a climate that the average Babylonian wouldn't give a fig for!

In conclusion, this country's distant, perhaps golden past, deserves much greater attention than it receives. Maybe this compilation of Essex sites is a step in that direction, hopefully to spur others into similar tasks in other counties of such revealing depths.

Ambresbury Banks

Prehistoric sites defined

These structures are found across the whole of Britain. Some do not appear in Essex but are mentioned for the sake of completeness.

Earthworks

British earthworks fall into three distinct categories; the causeway camp, the henge and the earth bank hill fort. The term 'earthwork' is used because it is sometimes difficult to distinguish between them because hill forts are often conversions of the earlier two. Also, maps are prone to misleading titles such as 'camp' and even 'castle' due to lack of information, that can cause the unwary to imagine a military encampment or a medieval fortress.

Causeway camps are the earlier of the trio. From around 4000 BC, these hill top enclosures consist of one or more concentric ringing ditches with the excavated material forming an inner bank or banks. These are disrupted by undug entrance causeways. About a dozen have been found in southern England, the most well known being Windmill Hill, Wilts, after which a sub-culture was named. Excavations make it evident that they were not occupied on a permanent basis. Pot shards and axe heads only tell us that traders travelled some distance to ply their wares. Conventionally they are thought to have been cattle pens or maybe religious meeting places or for medieval type fairs, but their function is very unclear.

From a Feng Shui angle they may have corresponded with the Chinese practice of physically altering the landscape to induce a finer balance of ch'i. Dowsers claim that energies flow in a circular motion around the banks. A combination of steep bank and a water filled ditch would at least serve as mediums for yin and yang mei lines.

With geomantic considerations in mind a popular view is that the sites were selected by a geomancer-equivalent who detected cross-over streams or blind springs and/or a fair balance of ch'i. Once reshaped the area would then be beneficial to practitioners of what we now might term 'occult' endeavours, from holistic healing to meditation or the enhancement of any psychic faculty.

Henges more than likely served the same ends. These appeared at about 2500 BC, and may have superseded the camps. They are often on flatter ground and are more common in the eastern half of England. The earth bank of a henge is piled on the outer side of the ditch with mostly single causeways. Inside, they differ in often having a ring of posts or stones. Stonehenge is the most famous although the henge breaks the rule by having the ditch and bank the 'wrong way round'. Marden, Wilts, is about the largest with a diameter of about 1600 feet. Avebury is a little smaller. Again, their purpose is a mystery.

So called hill forts are of the later Iron Age period too young to be associated with the time span we are concerned with. They are defensive in nature and more than likely had a rimming stockade and heavy gates across the causeways, or had foot bridges. They are set on high promontories or plateaus. The best known is Maiden Castle in Dorset. This enormous venture covers 100 acres with much of this consisting of triple banks and ditches of 70 foot depth.

Despite an elaborate jumble of banks at either end, objections are raised to the idea of Maiden Castle being solely defensive. It is not improbable that to defend such an enormous site a good 250,000 men would have been required. The Romans apparently stormed it which might reflect that this quantity was by then beyond the capacity of the area to provide.

If it had been a causeway camp then man-power was not a required factor. The later Iron Age militants probably found earlier earthworks fairly ideally situated and of a viable size so as to negate the need to build from scratch.

Essex has some two dozen earthworks ranging in size from 150 to 1900 feet across. Included are two causeway camps at

Springfield and Orsett. Six are on either side of the River Roding on high ground. Another cluster stretches from Pleshey across to Bishops Stortford. Nearly a quarter are on flat marsh land in the east flanking the Thames and the Crouch. In addition half a dozen henges may have existed.

Condition-wise they range from the difficult to find to those of grand impressive impact. Recommended sites to visit are Ambresbury and Loughton in Epping Forest, the Springfield camp, Sutton camp, Pleshey, Littlebury and the colossal Wallbury near Bishops Stortford.

Holy and beacon hills

Although they may now be devoid of any topping edifice many hills are considered to be special or holy in the eyes of folk tradition. Up until very recent times many were the focus of fairs and festivals such as Easter egg rolling; Glastonbury and St. Michael's Mount in the west country are prime examples. Thanks to their commanding views they evolved into fire beacon hills for signalling. Many are surmounted by churches to give an indication of a religious past.

In Essex we have St. Michael's Mount at Pitsea with it's ruined church atop. The St. Michael dedication is common on hill crest venues. In the light of feng shui it is perhaps no surprise that this saint is associated with dragons which in turn are linked with terrestrial energies, especially on hill tops. Near-by, the beacon hill at Canewdon is also an example of a pagan place, it and the church and village immersed in tales of witches, magic, ghosts and strange phenomena.

In China, hills like these had their crests shaped to conform to required secondary ch'i elements, labelled as fire, water, earth, metal and wood. Out holy hills could well have been altered to dictate the type of building that was erected or the activity thereon.

Plumberow Mount

Barrows and mounds

Over 40,000 of these earth domes exist in Britain. They cover a period from neolithic times up to the Saxons with many of the older examples being re-used over the millenniums. Sizes and shapes vary considerably. Most are known as bell and bowl barrows which are the familiar mounds. But there are saucer and pond barrows being respectively like low inverted saucers and an actual depression in the ground. Larger, bell shaped barrows are often passage graves having corbelled, roofed, stone block chambers accessible via a narrow passage.

The finest example is New Grange in Ireland, the oldest man-made structure in the world - save for maybe the Sphinx. It's 36 feet high and 280 across with a revetment of large stones. Like many others, especially on Anglesea, they include stones with enigmatic carvings of spirals, chevrons and zig-zags upon them. New Grange's passage also aligns with the rising sun at the winter solstice.

Related to round barrows are long barrows in which the burial area consists of three giant upright stones with an overlaying fourth member. Another form of long barrow, such as West Kennet, Wiltshire, are called gallery graves. Here, a stone lined passage at one end feeds several side galleries. A mystery with these earth mounds is that the chambers occupy a small fraction of the overall length , the bulk of the construction being apparently irrelevant. At West Kennet the bank is 330 feet long. These chalk and soil mounds also taper so that the stone-end is often twice the height of the far end. The material is dug from a rimming ditch. About 260 long barrows still survive. Cairns are round barrows of stone boulders found in the north of England and Scotland.

Not all barrows have burials, however, to compound mystery. Some, such as Silbury Hill and Merlin's Mount, Wiltshire, covers several acres and are the largest man made edifices in Europe.

What is also interesting is that most comprise of alternating layers of organic and inorganic material such as chalk, turf, earth and gravel. In the 1950s a psycho-therapist named Wilhelm Reich concluded that retained emotional and muscular tension in the human body could be linked to an unrecognised energy flow, that he referred to as orgone. He concluded that it was also present everywhere. Researchers now equate it to ch'i and nwyvre. Reich set up a lab' in the USA and built an orgone accumulator which was a box in which one could sit. The walls were of alternative organic and inorganic substances. They were found to assist the healing process of the body. But unfortunately his work was not accepted and he died before he could fully explore his theories. Reich knew nothing about British barrows nor did anybody recognise their composition at the time.

In Tom graves book, *Needles of Stone*, he speculates that tumuli could actually have been used to control rainfall. The basic principle was that the barrow might accumulate this orgone/ch'i which can be discharged into the sky to affect cloud polarity via a subterranean stream and adjacent standing stone where internal quartz would act a semi-conductor. It is an interesting hypothesis that has yet to be researched.

Essex has some 15 tumuli scattered all over the county. All are either saucer, bell or bowl types of various size. Many could be of the Neolithic period but is is known that the group at Bartlow are Roman as is Barrow Hill on Mersey Island.

Holy wells
Due to their practical importance as a village's often only supply of clean water, wells and springs would be expected to attract a degree of veneration, but many go a stage further. Not withstanding claimed healing properties, many wells have associations that cannot be tied in with practicalities. We are familiar with wishing wells, but what have wells got to do with making a wish? Some wells are called Holy Well. Some are said to connect certain buildings via a tunnel, reminiscent with legends associated with stones and earthworks where ley lines are invariably found. In pagan terms wells are symbolic of the entrance to mother earth and the underworld.

Holy wells are usually dedicated to Christian saints, mostly commonly to Helen and Ann. These are sanctified pagan goddesses, Ellen and Annus respectively. In Celtic mythology Ellen emerged from the underworld. Female deities are said to be well guardians. Some springs and wells are linked to other characters of the pagan pantheon like hobgoblins, Norse or Roman gods and goddesses.

In magical lore water is considered to be yin, lunar and female. Dowsers have often found networks of sub-terranean streams beneath stone circles, which in Feng Shui terms would be a conduit for yin energy. In terms of ch'i balance a favourable level might be found in yang dominated landscape that has a strong spring bursting up amidst it.

Essex has few holy wells. North Ockenden and Runwell are the two worth a visit.

Mazes

The maze or labyrinth, although of a different nature to stone and earth structures are also of the same era in origin. The oldest known design is inscribed on an Egyptian tomb of 3400 BC. The most famous could be the legendary Cretan maze wherein it is possible to get lost, as a choice of routes is presented. If you happen to be one of seven Cretan virgins then the idea is exactly that, followed by a nasty encounter with a minotaur if not rescued by Theseus!

The unicursal type of labyrinth is usually round, octagonal or square, but has a single serpentine course where the object would seem to focus on the actual walking in them. These grace church floor tiles, village greens as patterns in the turf and as rock carvings. The design is found abroad on Etruscan vases and on the walls of Hopi Indian dwellings, for example.

The purpose behind them is still a mystery. In the Middle Ages monks would complete the spiralling course on their knees in penance. Folklore suggests that the original objective was to enhance some mental faculty. Possibly the function of the Cretan maze was to develop the memory or intuition to a level where the practitioner could reach the centre and back without taking a wrong turn.

If geomantically positioned we may have a means of affecting an altered state of consciousness. Certainly Glastonbury Tor is a sacred site, and aerial photography has revealed that the ridges around it could have formed a seven-band, three dimensional, spiral maze. We might speculate that walking labyrinths back and forth in a decreasing spiral within an energy field might interact with corresponding neural energies enhancing certain abilities.

I have personally witnessed the Saffron Waldon labyrinth giving people a mild headache, myself included, and to also cause them to become disorientated. Sometimes it brings about various unexpected emotions on completion, or acts as a mild energy drain.

Britain may once have had hundreds of mazes and labyrinths, but only a handful survive, one in Essex.

Castles
Castles as such only date from the Normans but as with hill forts some were built on ancient pagan sites. In Essex, Colchester, Castle Hedingham, Saffron Walden and Hadleigh are the main venues.

Dene holes and groves
Just a few southern English counties can boast dene holes. The name is misleadingly derived from the word, Dane - and often pronounced as such, stemming from the theory that they were dug as hide-away repositories for belongings during Viking raids. This explanation is no more tenable than several others assigned to these deep, subterranean chambers accessed by vertical shafts.

The opinion that they were chalk mines seems fair enough. But the Grays dene holes, for example, are close to a surface source of this material ruling out that explanation, it would seem. The shafts empty into a chamber feeding dozens of further chambers arranged like the petals of a flower. Nothing is found in them that might lend a clue to the date of excavations.

The origins of groves are attributed to the Celts who landed here from the continent some 500 years before the Romans, although, settling without any major friction having come in small tribes, and with a similar culture to the natives. The priesthood were known as druids who later made their mark in history by a final defensive stand against the Roman legions on the Isle of Anglesea.

With their habit of submitting knowledge to memory our sum total of information on them comes from the conqueror's quills. They tell that they worshipped stones, wells, trees and the like, and held religious meetings in circular groves of oak. These sacred sites were deliberately planted trees that were continuously replaced over the centuries, and subsequently used by followers of a like belief perhaps right up to relatively recent times.

It is possible that these tree rings were initially planted on earlier venerated sites or that druids deployed similar methods of finding suitable spots as did the neolithic peoples.

Stone circles and standing stones
Because they represent the central theme of Neolithic construction, circles have been described already. What can be added here is that the majority of books on circles invariably fail to elaborate as to why none are found in the eastern counties. Because no circles have been found they tend to assume that none ever existed, citing that no natural outcrops of stone are available. But close study of the area suggests otherwise. There are no outcrops but there are numerous stones.

Beauchamp Roding

In Essex there is no proof that a given stone is a glacial erratic or that it was not dragged in from afar as with the Stonehenge bluestones. Furthermore, post Bronze Age peoples would assimilate stone from circles into their buildings when a natural supply was lacking. In the west of England with its plentiful natural supply, the raiding of stone rings would be less of a necessity.

Evidence may also lay in the fact that geographically, sites such as Alphamstone and Gestingthorpe, together with say, Ingatestone and Arkesden occupy the same kind of terrain as circles elsewhere. None are at the type of location where these rings are not found, that is on flat marshy ground, so prevalent in eastern England. North-West of the Roman road that is now the A12 we find hilly folds embedded with river lined valleys so favoured by neolithic builders for stone erecting.

Watkins referred to standing stones on leys as mark stones, merely marking the track of a ley. Today researchers tend to see them playing an active rather than a passive role in the ley network. However, some stones may simply be markers, especially where leys cross. This might explain stones in low lying places under which dowsers find no evidence of streams, etc, to activate them.

With regards to finding stones, we must also be aware of the several uses that they have been given since Saxon times, serving to complicate identification. They can be used for rubbing stones for cattle and mounting blocks were common in days of equine travel, and so many have been moved, if ancient in origin, from their prime repose.

Parishes were set up by the Anglo-Saxons for tithing and boundary purposes marked with stones. The problem with finding a boundary stone is; what came first, the stone or the boundary. Was the stone moved or was the boundary delineated in accord to the stone's position?

Stones may have been set up to mark market places where they became an 'omphalos' or sacred centre from which crossroads emanate to the four directions, as at Royston in Hertfordshire. Again, it must be defined as to whether the stone is in its original place.

Standing stones feature prominently in rural folklore. Various edicts were promulgated by the Church for centuries forbidding stone worship. Stones are given names. Legends often refer to their 'magical' aspects whereby a stone that is moved to serve another purpose, such as fording a stream, is found to be mysteriously unsuitable. Then it will take a single horse to haul the block uphill to where it belonged as opposed to three horses in the down hill direction. The puddingstone at Standon, Herts, is said to rotate three times at midnight and go down to the River Rib to drink. This typical legend varies subtly usually by substituting the time for May Day, sunrise or when the cock crows.

Healing properties are attributed to them where-by the patient would walk around one three times backwards, slide down it or, if hollow, such as Men an Tol, Cornwall, crawl through it. Another way is to drink water poured over it.

Stones can be found where three ways meet; these being sacred places where people congregated. Churchyards often came complete with a pillar. Foundation stones originated in churches due to papal decrees ordering the use of pagan sites. Some of the site stones were broken up for wall material but some were obviously so venerated that they were left untouched or had the church built over them even to the extent of them being an obtrusive obstacle, such as at Eastwood church. Braintree and Broomfield churches have stones poking out of their outer walls.

Numerous stones can be found near farm buildings. The field searcher must be wary here because most are the result of deep ploughing. The stone was then subsequently dumped on grass verges to prevent parking, as show pieces or wall corner protectors. Clues to the ancient use of them should be sought.

Look to see if the farm frontage is close to a three ways meet. Examine the boulder to see if it appears to have centuries of wear that might preclude it having been a recent buried find. If the said monolith is on a ley line this could be a reasonable clue to an ancient placing. None of the 'farm' stones that I have personally found to be plough finds are on leys.

In favour, however, of a dug stone being of sacred lineage is the fact that during the 'stone killing' puritan purges many stones were deliberately buried in what are now fields, to be later rediscovered.

Essex has no grand stone of the likes of the monsters of Wessex but a few are the height of a man (if stood up). However, for a county that is invariably excluded from the stone culture stamping ground, there is quite an abundance of them. Although some could be lifted by one man on average they are a bit more imposing. In all, 100 plus sites have been identified, several with numerous stones would total many tons.

Distribution conforms to where we would expect to find them if using the rule of thumb of other counties and if applying Feng Shui principles in their siting. Only a few are found in the flat East. Of these Chadwell surmounts a sudden ridge supplying the yang to the surrounding yin energy. Likewise, Thundersley's Bird stone rest upon a sudden thrust of a ridge to command a surprising vista. Indeed, as with earthworks and tumuli in what we think of as flat areas, the visitor is so often amazed at the view.

Boxted and Dedham are situated amidst pronounced rises of land sweeping up from river valleys. Only Bulpham, Hawkwell and Eastwood occupy flat terrain, if by no means marshy. They could, however, be true mark stones in the Watkins sense passively marking a ley that they all stand on.
Of the other monoliths and fragments they lie to the west of a line delineated by the Roman road from London to Braintree then from there to Sudbury with a few stretching east along the Colne and Stour valleys. They are well scattered with slight

concentrations around Chipping Ongar and a zone just south of Saffron Walden. I personally doubt that this is a chance affair. If they were all glacial erratics then surely we would find them more evenly dispositioned.

Preaching crosses

Also called teaching and market crosses, these are stone pillars carved with head crosses or deities and Christian orientated art work. They are mostly found in Cornwall but also all over Britain if thinning out in the East. Early examples were standing stones subjected to the converting chisel, and most date from Saxon times. They were the forerunners of churches, and once the latter began to appear they marked consecrated ground and stood midway between the gate and the south porch and slightly east. After the Reformation of the 16th century the carving was discontinued.

The shafts are circular and rectangular and the tableau designs can also be Celtic or Danish, featuring whorls and geometric patterns or the enigmatic interlacing knotwork that could represent interweaving terrestrial energies with no beginning and no end. Fertility vines are also found, along with animals, human figures and leaves.

I have located only three in Essex. One at Castle Hedingham is a full length shaft. Little Burstead has two pieces of a base stone, and a small piece is embedded in the church wall at Saffron Walden.

Chapter Two

Church paganism

The common image of an English parish church is of a picturesque yet staid, austere building dedicated in design to reflect the sombre devotions of those within. The advance of civilisation has tarnished many a quiet pastoral setting but most of the hallowed sanctuaries remain. But if we take a closer look at these edifices we may be in for a surprise. Despite much rebuilding and alteration over the centuries enough is left to reveal that in the Middle Ages, when most were erected, these buildings were radically different to our perception of them. The base structure remains unaffected but very few decorative features lent anything to Christian ideology. Today's 'white washed' and erased churches are but a pale shadow of their former glory.

Churches came complete with lavish, coloured murals and other designs that extended to the pillars, arches and ceilings. Stained glass embellished most windows, and liberally spread carvings of lurid shades took the form of hideous gargoyles, sexually explicit figures that would be considered pornographic today, heretical symbolism and writhing dragons being killed or eating people! Peruse the remaining remnants and we may realise that by modern standards we might accurately use the word bizarre to describe them.

This throws a completely new light on our conception of religious and secular life of the past. Church design could well reflect on another picture we nurture of early times whereby practically the whole village would devotedly parade through the local church porch every Sunday and Holy day to chorus familiar hymns with faithful verve. This may have been far from the

Great Canfield

truth. The entire ecclesiastical question is much more diverse and complicated than we are led to believe by clergy and guide book. Indeed, these sources of information almost seem to conspire to uphold a biased illusion. Seldom do the guide books mention the carvings, and if so doing decline to elaborate. Interpretations are often grossly inaccurate or misleading. Colleagues and I have found that the clergy will sometimes even try to steer you off the subject of pagan carvings, if broached. Those who will discuss them often know nothing or are not even aware of the existence of given examples.

But delve into the history of the Church and it is hardly surprising to find the situation we have today. For one, people always talk of 2000 years of the Church. This is an exaggeration considering that it was not formed until the 4th century and not introduced to these shores for another 200 years. Allegiances of Essex kings then shows that consolidation was by no means secured.

During times when politics and religion went hand in glove the latter was little more than a government department aimed at controlling people via threats of eternal damnation, gathering tithes and boosting the wealth and influence of its hierarchy.

In it's founding years under the Romans the empire periodically adopted a fresh religion through expedience to pander to the changing whims of the electorate. Christianity was cunningly malleable, constantly modifying to suit the flavour of the day, often by absorbing elements of rival faiths. In Britain the Celts had their own long established beliefs, and old habits die hard. Conversions were usually gained by bribery, the sword, and by outlawing opposing activities such as tree worship. In Rome special offers were made to slaves. One such deal was a one off chance to come over to the Lord on a chosen Sunday and in so doing gain their freedom! The rush must have topped the January sales at Markus and Spensus! At other times adherents paid less taxes and were under the protection of the army - not so if of pagan persuasion.

Actually, most folk were, and still are, not really 'religious' so any fad or incentive would cause them to adhere to, or abandon, a faith like changing a soap powder. One English king converted to stop his Christian wife from nagging him! And in those days if the king changed his faith then hoards of his subjects followed suit. The notion of the savage pagan swiftly seeing the light is a fallacy. It was only the advent of urbanised technology that severed the British from their roots and finally defeated earth harmonising paganism - well almost!

Historical records show that the Church suffered from long persisting teething troubles. In 601 AD Pope Gregory dispatched a letter to St Augustine via the Abbe Melitus instructing him to; 'by no means destroy the temples of the idols belonging to the English, but only the gods which are found in them; let holy water be sprinkled over them, in as much as those temples are well constructed it is necessary that they should be converted from the ownership of demons to the true God.'

Edicts were constantly needed to ban pagan gatherings at their temples, stones, wells and three way meets. King Cnut, who features prominently in Essex history, made such a decree in 1035.

All the major Christian festivals are renamed adaptions of other religious occasions. Christmas is the Celtic Yule Sabbat and the Roman Saturnalia feast. December 25th is also the birthday of Mithras, a solar god of the Persians. Easter is filched from the German fertility goddess, Eostre. Easter bunnies, eggs and hot cross buns are pagan, representing fertility and the sun, the cross on the bun being the equal armed Celtic design. Mayday is Beltaine, a Celtic fire festival. Even Guy Fawkes night is a transposition of Samhain/Hallowe'en of November 1st, the start of the Celtic year, a Sabbat when the Gates of Annwn are open allowing the spirits of the dead into this world, spirits that are not supposed to be evil 'goblins'. The concept of the resurrection is a fusion of the revival of spring and the story of Ishtar the Babylonian goddess of the underworld.

The Christian disparaging attitude towards sex stems from the need to outlaw some of the fundaments of pagan ritual, and with this objective they dreamed up the concept of the devil, using the Greek god Pan, and pagan horned gods, as his image, hence gaining the features of a goat. Occult arts became the work of the devil. The mythological pantheon of the Britons became the minions of Satan.

With this in mind we might expect churches to reflect it. A situation appeared to exist where the ruling classes supported the Church whilst the country pagans - pagan stems from the latin paganus, meaning country dweller - were the parishioners and the actual builders. Carvings illustrate the early fusion of faiths and influence of paganism. Unfortunately carvings have shed their meanings to the passage of years to leave us with one of the multiple aspects of earth mysteries.

Let us now cast an eye over these 'works of the devil' that for reasons now lost were accepted into the fabric of these temples of worship. They lurk in several forms. The names that I have ascribed to them, if used elsewhere, are fairly arbitrary because most types bear several common traits. They are described as gargoyles, grotesques, green men, dragons, animals, tongue pokers, mouth pullers, solar carvings and paintings.

Attempts at further analysis can invite confusion. Tongue pokers and mouth pullers are basically gargoyles and grotesques which in turn are closely related. 'Devils' could be considered as a separate type but I have listed them as grotesques. Animals come as accurate depictions of pigs and cats etc, and also as semi human beasts with face distorting overtones. Some animals are mythical such as the phoenix or griffin. Some appear to be hybrid species or a bad attempt at an unfamiliar animal. Dragons come in varied forms, often with aspects of other carvings.

Gargoyles and grotesques
The word gargoyle is from the French, meaning 'water spout' which reflects the functional purpose. As such they line gutters

Great Dunmow

shedding rain water through their mouth pipes. Grotesques have no function and are found inside and out but bear no real artistic difference to gargoyles.

In style they display a wide diversity. In size the full bodied versions range from a small cat to an Alsation dog. What they represent is not known, although they probably adhered to a set theme. Within this, individual masons could have had free reign of their imagination. They don't appear to represent any of the pagan gods as such. It seems as if masons competed with each other to see who could come up with the ugliest monster because some look like escapees from a nightmare or the inhabitants of an LSD trip! One official explanation is that they are evil spirits banished to the outside of the church. But the problem here is that many are on the inside. Another offer is that they are meant to scare off evil spirits. But as they look like evil spirits aren't they more liable to attract them?

Their survival today poses one of the minor mysteries concerning the purges of the puritans with their abhorrence to idols. During the 17th century iconaclists had orders to go on a vandalistic rampage destroying anything that their prudish minds found offensive.

One such man was William Dowsing who paid visits to Suffolk churches proudly exclaiming that in one day he did; 'brake down 1000 superstitious pictures in stained glass.' I've not found one window that could be considered as offensive or superstitious so I wonder as to the content of the numerous panes of old.

Many Essex churches show evidence of obliteration on this scale, yet some survive almost totally unscathed. Were they missed thanks to sheer weight of numbers - Essex has over 380. It does not appear that orders were directed to each parish, unless it was up to the discretion of each rector as to what was destroyed. Maybe the purge was more or less completed in that only the more offensive carvings were targeted. If so medieval churches may have been even more outlandish than remaining evidence suggests. If Sheela-na-gig exhibitionists and some phallic animals survive, the mind boggles as to the nature of extinct examples of that ilk.

Did the scores of carvings at Thaxted, for example, survive because they got through the net on account of not being too unacceptable? In reverse, most of the grotesque heads at places like Rochford have been battered to bits, yet appear to resemble survivors which are not controversial. Did the demise of a gargoyle depend on how long a ladder they could find at a given church? Did rich parishioners pay off the wreckers? The prominent parishes of Great Dunmow, Great Waltham and Saffron Walden have no perceivable damage whilst smaller places suffered.

Green men

These are human male heads with foliage sprouting from the ears, mouth and nose, or heads peering through foliage or consisting of it. The style stems from Roman times and probably represents the fructifying energy that causes the countryside to blossom in spring. They may represent dryads, tree elementals of folklore. Little men of the forest named woodwoses are another possibility. Green men are quite distinctive and only share their traits with a few dragons and animals. They may also be symbolic of death, making the statement that we return to the earth but new life sprouts from old, emphasising the eternal cycle of nature.

Parallels to these carvings are the Jack-in-the-Green figures of May Day festivals still re-enacted today. Here, a man wears a wooden conical framework covered with greenery through which he peers. He is also known as King-of-the-May and various names such as Jack-in-the-Bush and Robin-of-the-Wood. This is the figure usually depicted on signs board of Green Man pubs, reminding us of Robin Hood. This semi-legendary hero is probably a personification of the green man who in turn stands for the old religion, in this instance. The clash between the merry men and the Sheriff of Nottingham may well be an allegorical tale stemming from the friction between the two beliefs, being as

Robin gives to the poor - the pagans - what he steals from the rich - the Church.

In British mythology the green man corresponds with Cernunnos and Herne the Hunter, both forest deities.

Essex churches house a fair thicket of green men, the most notable being at Bulmer, Hedham, Mucking, South Ockenden and Widdington.

Tongue pokers and mouth pullers

These are grotesque and gargoyle heads with protruding tongues or with hands pulling the mouth open, or 'pulling a face' unaided. The tongue can be anatomically normal or grossly long and distorted. Mouth pullers follow suit. Both types are a mystery but might be 'cleaned up' versions of the more blatantly sexual carving known as Sheela-na-gigs.

It is wondered if the act of poking the tongue out and pulling the mouth is considered a rude gesture because it is in imitation of these fertility carvings. we may find they are based on earlier religious statues that expose exaggerated genitals in a gesture meant to keep evil spirits out of the house, the pose being a vulgar way of saying 'go away'.

The Church's explanation for the tongue poker is that it is a warning against sinning as they are supposed to depict a hanged man where the tongue often lolls out. However, the facial expressions do not always tally, and some animals, like pigs, also share this feature, so unless they hung pigs for stealing in days of old..?

Essex has about 15 churches with worthy examples, notably at Henham, Foxearth, Sheering, Stebbing, Terling and Thaxted.

Sheering

Dragons

Essex has about 30 churches with dragons in wood, stone and glass. Perhaps the best are at Ardleigh, Bowers Gifford, Copford, Fobbing, Great Bromley, Great Waltham, Goldhanger, Henham, Tilty and Wormingford.

In Britain we generally associate this mythical beast with St George and to a lesser extent St. Michael and St. Margaret who also slew them. These opposing factions are frequently evident in our churches. The origins of this symbolism are obscure, although it was the Crusaders who discovered the tomb of George, an obscure martyre, in the Holy land and adopted him because the wars were not going too well. They won the next battle so they promoted him to a saint who then replaced the older dragon slayer, the biblical St. Michael, a more complicated figure.

As opposed to other countries, the British dragon is seen as a symbol of evil, the biblical serpent and the devil. However, these concepts were invented by the Church for propaganda purposes. To the pagan population it represented elemental forces, as it does elsewhere in the world. The Chinese ch'i travels along what are dubbed dragon paths. The yang energy aspect is portrayed by an azure dragon. So the beast is considered to be a fortuitous and beneficial creature associated with basic cosmic elements.

St. George spearing the dragon is seen as symbolic of the victory of the new religion over pagan beliefs. However, many researchers wonder if the depiction is not quite as simple as that. As at Wormingford, the dragon is often shown on a leash, not being speared. It has been suggested that the root of the name, George, is geo, meaning, of the earth, hence the name could be a corruption of 'urger of the earth'.

It could be that the saint is not killing the beast - or was not originally - but is securing it, controlling or 'tapping into it'. The action of piercing it with a spear or sword could be misleading and so eventually misunderstood. The dragon depicts energy, not a live animal, so no harm would be done.

Great Waltham

In some dragons the terrestrial energy theme is apparent in that they issue greenery from their mouths like green men. Some have their tails terminate as leaves as at Tilty and Goldhanger. That they symbolise something of great value can be gauged by their role in mythology, especially in China and Scandinavia where they are guardians of royalty, pearls of wisdom and treasure.

Church dragons come in several styles as they do the world over. Notable is the North European and Greek form; the wyvern, from a Saxon word meaning serpent. This version has only two legs, which are of an eagle, wings and a curly tail. The four legged dragon is common and usually minus the characteristic, heraldic arrow-head tail that was acquired in the 17th century. Some features heads which are lizard-like or even look like that of a dog of a man. Others are bodily like lizards or fierce worm/snake creatures.

Exhibitionists

This term is applied to what are called sheela-na-gigs and the less frequent male versions. This carving is now rare in Britain with less than 40 remaining. Ireland fares better with around 75. This rarity is no surprise because they consist of a woman, usually of hag appearance, with her hands holding open her genitals! The Normans appear to have brought the design to this land from France and Spain where many also exist. We can be fairly certain that they are not meant to be erotic or obscene. Today's attitudes to sex are radically different to what it was in the past. She is probably an earth mother figure or even an encouragement to reproduce in an age when the human survival rate was no comparison to today. To have many children meant that your family survived. The Sheela-na-gig at Whittlesford in Cambs has a phallic half-man half-animal with her.

Unfortunately Essex has but one of these figures left, and is detached, if safe enough, in Colchester Castle museum.

Great Waltham

Animals

Animal carvings come in conventional form or in mythical guise such as the griffin or phoenix, and as various hybrids. We must first be aware that three animals, the winged bull, lion and the eagle, together with an angel are Christian depictions of the four apostles. However, they are relatively uncommon compared with the number of pagan examples such as the pig, stag, cat, boar, monkey, hare, lion, cow, bat, fox and bear. Sheep, goats and dogs are also less common.

Horned beasts may stem from the horned god Cernunnos. Ceridwen, the goddess of inspiration, who became the archetypal witch, is known as the sow goddess, so pigs could relate to her. The monkey may be an Egyptian influence being the god Thoth/Tehuti the god of judgement, science and wisdom, shown with a baboon's head. Lions had probably become familiar via bible stories and may have been symbolic of strength as is found at Sheering, Essex. Boars and hares both feature in Celtic mythology. The phoenix is likely to represent the resurrection of life in spring or retain one of it's many, age old, foreign meanings. Some animals have foliage emissions like green men.

Essex has a fair share of animals in its churches, some of the best being at Ardleigh, Great Canfield, Great Waltham, Henham, Little Dunmow, Lindsell, Sheering, Stebbing, Saffron Walden and Thaxted.

Solar carvings

Evidence of sun worship and solar deities are evident in church decoration. One of the most familiar is the radial sun burst of Norman tympanums above doors. Others include solar wheels, human faced suns called hagodays, swastikas and various other heavenly symbols resulting from religious influences of the Romans and, at the time, the crusaders returning from the middle east.

Essex has some fine examples, notably at Abbess Roding, Great Canfield, Fryerning, Little Laver and Saffron Walden.

Paintings
Parish churches when built, had their interiors lavishly muralled with symbols and biblical scenes, etc. But puritanical purges saw that very few have survived, and most of these are of 'innocent' Christian themes. But a few display pagan overtones such as the zodiac at Copford, astrology being later banned as heretical.

Essex paintings, expansive or traces, can be found at Colchester (St Leonards), Copford, Little Tey, Little Braxted, Tilbury Juxta Clare and Waltham.

Chapter Three

Discovering ley lines

In a sentence, ley lines are straight alignments of structures built by prehistoric man. If they do exist then they are literally an interlacing aspect of the other facets of earth mysteries.

Their discovery is credited to a Herefordshire businessman, Alfred Watkins. Born in 1855 he became a School Governor, JP, County councillor, a Fellow of the Royal Photographic Society, and inventor of photographic equipment. He was President of the Woolhope Naturalist Field Club, local dignitary and supporter of worthy causes. All in all he was the essence of the English Edwardian gentleman, and no doubt considered to be a jolly decent chap by all who crossed his path during his frequent travels.

Actually Watkins was not the type of person we would expect to be connected with the unconventional. But he was a mild eccentric who hob-nobbed with characters whom his wife frowned upon when invited home to tea. It was from these rustic country folk that he learned the local legends and folklore pertaining to the stones and earthworks he frequented. In 1921, at the age of 66, he was idly gazing at a map whilst sitting in his new-fangled motor car when he had an 'inspirational flash of vision', to become aware of a network of inter-linking straight lines between ancient sites.

Watkins carried out tests and discovered that they were well above the chance factor. He published his findings four years later, initially terming the lines, leys, from a Saxon word that often cropped up in place names on the lines, meaning a clearing or tract of unploughed land. He perceived them as ancient track

Bulpham

ways but then disgarded the term ley in favour of old straight track, as is evident in the title of his book and the club he founded to investigate them.

He died in 1935. His club finally folded in the late forties, no doubt to the satisfaction of conventional archaeology that had never accepted the idea with its occult overtones. This attitude is only today beginning to fade. But in the new post war age of atomic enlightenment it was not considered to stand much chance of rearing it's head again.

However, peculiar objects in the sky began to appear, to be dubbed flying saucers. This phenomena was viewed as a public fad destined to die a natural death - as did leys. But whatever flying saucers were they didn't go away, but kept coming to spawn world-wide UFO investigation groups and a continued controversy. By the early sixties the subject was diversifying and a theory arose that UFOs flew along the 're-discovered' ley lines. The idea was soon dropped but it left Watkins' leys in full view of a generation with fresh ideas, ironically as a reaction to the atomic age. A wave of adherents was the result.

So let us look at ley line sites. These 'points' are those constructed or utilised during the Neolithic and Bronze Age cultures responsible for stone circles, henges, long barrows and causeway camps. It ended at around 1500 BC after thriving for some 2000 years or more. They are the oldest extant monuments in the British Isles and maybe the world. Ley points also consist of medieval ecclesiastical buildings on pagan sites.

Stone circles are considered to be the core of the ley network if only due to their superior complexity. It is to be noted that there are none now known in eastern England where leys exist, but long ago this may well have not been the case. Circles appear to be the functional perpetrators of leys, at least if you adhere to the 'earth energy' school of thought. Single menhirs may have tapped energy, and/or have been used as markers as Watkins perceived. Essex has no circles but over 90 single stones that could have once been active.

In the field, if found on a ley a lone stone frequently appears to have been placed there of old. A 'genuine' stone can sometimes be identified by dint of their shape. Some actually 'point' along the ley or have one side 'shaved' flat as a directional indicator.

Henges and causeway camps, that are rare in Essex, can lend a clue to a ley's presence, too. A common tendency is for leys to run along the rim of the ditch rather than pass through the centre of the enclosure. Leys that hit the centre may do so because the site had been extended in the Iron age to become a hill fort, or castle base at a later date. Pleshey in Essex is a good example. Where this 'rule' is broken I have found that the ley almost always terminates at the site rather than continuing on.

At holy and beacon hills leys mostly tend to pass over the highest point, probably aiming at a one time edifice, although the hill's intrinsic properties may have been the important factor. If a ley runs across the side of a hill then it is not usually to the detriment of visual sighting of the next site, a rule that leys conform to. If thinking in terms of active beaming of energy then high spots would be ideal for uninterrupted transmission.

Holy wells, springs and long and round barrows, called tumuli, would have to stand, due to their small size, fairly precisely on leys to be included. Check that they do if ley hunting.

Essex has one set of dene holes and one very recently discovered cursus. The Grays dene holes cover a few acres so ley siting here is flexible. If they were part of the system then maybe some central or nodal point once existed, maybe a lone, long gone stone. The two leys (that I have found) at Grays do stem from the same point.

Most cursus's are too large to conform to any narrow beam criteria in the manner of other sites. In Wessex leys appear to cross them at random. However, at Springfield in Essex the cursus has three leys that I have found that strike it at near enough dead centre and exactly at either end. This, however, may be just chance.

Finally, we have churches and abbeys to consider. In eastern counties these are the most numerous of sites. They have to have been built prior to the dissolution of the monasteries of 1536. At that date the practise of building on older pagan sites discontinued. It is not the church or priory, that we are concerned with, but the grounds in which they stand, or what is, or was in the grounds. If a plotted line actually misses a church it need not necessarily count as a 'miss'. Check the site in the field, it can be most rewarding to find that the church is, say, a few hundred feet from a flattened tumulus or battered mark stone in a ditch, or that the whole area is an artificially raised platform of earth. Imagine if the henge at Avebury circle had been almost destroyed and a ley on your map missed the church there - to be declared null and void as a ley site!

Also included by Watkins were sites that are now usually relegated to a secondary place as such. These are fords, ponds, tree clumps and cross roads. The devaluation is due to uncertainty about their age and because the founder perceived leys as literal trading tracks. Even he later realised that this was an impracticality. Leys cross all manner of impassable ground from bogs to crags, rivers to lakes. Watkins doubted his own hypothesis but could not envisage an alternative.

The Hereford man considered that leys were visually surveyed with the aid of long rods. The chalk hill figure at Wilmington, Sussex, is cited by some as one such surveyor. He is holding two long staves. Could it really be an echo of long gone times? Nightfall was thought to be no hindrance to surveying because sighting fires on beacon hills could be lit. Place names such as flash or flam are, as a result, associated with them, suggested Watkins. He also wondered if ponds and fords were used to reflect distant firelight and so aid aligning the sites. These fire related words are now thought to be the result of solar alignments on sites such as at Stonehenge.

The syllable, 'dod' found in ley sites names, was very neatly speculated as originating from the surveyor's 'doding' movement as he positioned his rods during sightings. Doddinghurst in

Essex is one such name. It may well be that we get the word doddery and dodge from this source, he suggested. A snail in some counties is called a Dodman because of its horns that resemble staffs. But it would seem doubtful if the word could have survived under the subsequent assault of modifying language. Today's English only stems back to the middle ages.

Of the word, ley, itself, in it's favour, the commonly accepted meaning of pasture or clearing does not always fit in with the places so named. The syllable often comes applied to a mountainous or swampy area. The term 'lay of the land' interestingly, refers to a survey. To 'lay a gun' ie an artillery piece, refers to a straight line. The name Crossley is odd because pastures can hardly be considered to cross one another. Then we have the old nursery rhyme; 'as I was going to Widdecombe fair, all along, out along, down a long lea...' Lea is one of several spellings. A village with the root word, cross, however, will invariably refer to a teaching or preaching cross.

Watkins found that lone tree clumps and single trees habitually marked the course of a ley. They may well have done so once but today none would still exist. The only redeeming probability is that people replaced the trees in accord with tradition, eventually unaware of their original purpose. I personally take note if these growths appearing on a prominent knoll or in a churchyard if they are of the species Pinus Silvestris, the Scots Pine, as Watkins noted, and probably used because they are evergreen and stand out against other trees.

Crossroads and places where three roads meet are worthy of investigation for signs of a mark stone, although it does not pay to go marking them as such willy nilly on the map. The value of a crossroad is maybe thanks to site evolution. A stone would require a path for access, so several might develop. Eventually the stone might vanish but the roads would remain to this day.

Most rural English roads can be traced back to the 11th century, so little modern change has occurred. Then, of course, some roads were originally Roman, often built on existing roads. In his book

Watkins mentions a funeral custom where the procession would halt at a crossroad - with no marker - and say a prayer because 'it has always been done'.

Although it is possible that stones were the cause of crossroad reverence, the latter appears to have an intrinsic value alone. Several cultures revere crossroads with little mention of stones. King Cnut banned meeting at these junctions - unless an unmentioned stone resided at them all. But Hecate is the Greek goddess of black magic - and crossroads of all things. As far as I know they were not marked with sacred stones in Greece. Hecate also had three faces and appeared at tombs and scenes of crimes. In Britain witches and suicides were traditionally buried at crossroads. The Romans believed that spirits called Lares dwelt at crossroads.

Moats are sometimes counted if they surround homesteads of the pre-reformation period. In Essex they commonly grace ley lines. The premise for inclusion is that the house or manor might have been established by a holy well or standing stone, etc.

To be treated as viable sites are buildings marked as Temple Farm or simply Templars, on maps. These points often play host to preceptories of the medieval order of military monks of the Knights Templar. As with other monastic orders they probably built on pagan venues.

Having drawn our linear network let us stand back and view it as a whole. No geometric patterns emerge. All we have is a seemingly random web of straight lines. We must take into account that they are not now complete, although nothing like a symmetric whole is evident.

Several leys in Essex, for example, run parallel with another. One in five of all Essex leys that I have plotted are of the same angle, three times higher than chance would allow. But I cannot see any significance in this as yet.

How long is a ley? How many points should be included? Watkins used the criteria of four in four miles or a minimum of five in around 20 miles. Originally it was probably all down to how many sites on a given stretch that were found suitable, so in theory some leys could only have two points.

Today we can only aim to exceed the chance factor by a comfortable margin. By chance a single O/S map sheet should produce frequent four pointers, if not of a four mile length. An early researcher, John Williams, has shown that a single sheet should throw up about two five pointers. By this criteria Essex should have about ten, yet I have found over 80 to date and some of these have actually eight points. Chances of a five pointer are about 250 to one against.

How wide is a ley? A question seldom asked. It would make sense if they were the width of the smallest point, which could be a stone or a well. If so, a stone circle would only 'pick up' a ley at one or two stones, and not at it's diametric whole. It may be worth noting that many circles have a few members that stand out from the herd in the form of outliers, centre stones and entrance stones. If the whole circle transmitted/received then some leys would be extremely wide if rings like Avebury and Stenness are considered, and then what of Stanton Drew with it's well spaced triple rings? Do leys widen or diminish depending on the monument they are approaching?

What about the other dimension? Leys are straight in the lateral plane but not in the horizontal. Ley points at different heights give a side view of zig zagging undulation. Is there a limit to the angle at which ley sections can meet? We may be able to find ancient edifices via ley plotting on maps, but what of finding leys in the field at the edifices? There are a few things we can look for. We have mentioned that place names can give a clue. What else? Look for a stretch of straight road leading to a church or stone, this can be following the path of a ley. At sites look to see if the next site is, or could have been visible. A notch in a distant hill will also sometimes give away a ley's course.

A valuable clue is found if a ley point has a legend of a tunnel running to the next site. Often these stories include a devil, cocks crowing, treasure or a crock of gold. So often the supposed tunnel would be impractically long, serve no purpose or be impossible to dig because the sub-strata would not allow it. These links may be distorted folk memories of a ley.

As to ley line benefits, a common misconception is that living on one will bestow the occupier with a whole heap of good fortune and splendid health. There is not, as far as I have discovered, any gain what-so-ever in residing on a ley. Maybe there once was, but the entire system is now in ruins so in theory it would not be functioning properly. Not that there is anything to suggest that lines were permanently 'live'. In fact, folklore would suggest that stone circles may have only been active at set times of the year, or when activated by the interaction with people. Tom Graves, in his book, *Needles of Stone*, also encourages us to think that the leys were paths for pulses of energy, enough at least to give the participants in the circle they experimented with a strong headache. So it maybe unwise to get in the way of an energy pulse, let alone live on one!

So what are leys? Let us attempt to run through the process of creating one on the strength of what we know. They connect stone, earth and water mediums and are dictated by fixed earth and water points, this we can feel safe to assume. It would appear that Neolithic man chose his sites on a similar basis to the Chinese geomancer, so we can imagine such adepts scouring the land using dowsing techniques in search of places where the dragon's veins beneficially cross. Then a venue might be modified to increase it's potential, maybe by digging henges and by asymmetric hill top reshaping. Many of these sites would be over blind springs that could be actual streams, dragon veins or geological fault lines. Wells with a higher than average energy concentration would also be sought.

At these propitious earth nodes would be erected a stone circle. Prehistoric man would need to be aware of the geographical inter-relationship of the sites, maybe they even had deer skin maps. If we accept the view that the ley system is a kind of national grid, then straight lines would be drawn on their map incorporating as many sites as coincidence would allow. At best a line would probably include only two or three points. So now our geomancers walk the lines - which are not yet 'proper' leys at this stage - seeking further sites of secondary strength and marking them with, maybe, a single stone. To enable an uninterrupted flow of energy, intermediate hills would acquire a 'pick up' stone, also. Further, single stones would mark the inactive places where leys happened to cross. Finally, they might seek to make use of the active network by constructing further henges and the like on the leys to reap their benefit. This is, of course, essentially my personal view.

Sample Essex leys described

The following are five Essex leys chosen on a distribution basis. The reference code system commences with two letters indicating the county in which they commence. EX, CB, HF, KT, SF, meaning Essex, Cambridgeshire, Hertfordshire, Kent and Suffolk respectively. The accompanying number is the magnetic angle of the ley using Grid North.

It is not known at which end a ley starts or finishes so I read them as if reading a book, that is, from the left end to the right. The numbers thus run at 01 to 179.5 degrees. Other counties are involved because leys have no respect for modern boundaries hence some leys do not commence or end in Essex. A small 'n' or 's' after the number refers to north and south, necessary because several leys have the same bearing. All the churches mentioned are parish churches of pre-reformation vintage.

SF106 Bartlow 154-486452 to Nayland 168-975340

A fairly long ley of seven points that starts and finishes in Suffolk but spends most of its time in Essex. From BARTLOW CHURCH it runs some nine miles before picking up at the RIDGEWELL STONE on the village green by the old water pump, so plenty of scope is left for intermediate field work, and the ley still works if Bartlow is dropped as being a chance point. From the stone it takes a very short trip to RIDGEWELL CHURCHYARD. A mile further on it passes through the 500 year old church of TILBURY JUXTA CLARE with its grotesque heads and winged beast. It then arrives at the crossroads at GESTINGTHORPE where several stones mark a garden and farm site. Passing into an area quite heavy with stone sites it hits GENTRY'S FARM to be joined by two further leys. Two thigh high stones lay here by a Vet's house on the Great Henny road. The adjacent field is called Golden Ley, as discovered on finding an embroidered map in Bulmer church, suggesting connections with solar align-ments and stones. The ley then crosses back into Suffolk to terminate at the earthwork at NAYLAND COURT KNOLL.

EX79n Tillingham Hall 177-622872 to Paglesham 178-927931
This ley possibly begins at a moat of TILLINGHAM HALL, a probable ancient site, before heading east to six more definite sites. The first is NORTH BENFLEET CHURCH where another ley, EX120.5, crosses en route to Thundersley church which is visible from the churchyard. EX79n then reached RAYLEIGH MOUNT where it clips the edge of the south side moat in typical fashion. From here the ley points become much closer, finding the Venus stone at HAWKWELL after a few miles, then a mile on HAWKWELL CHURCH. Half a mile on it crosses the site of the defunct preaching cross that stood at GOLDEN CROSS, Ashingdon, before winding up near the coast by clipping the northern edge of PAGLESHAM CHURCHYARD.

KT51 Sutton at Hone 177-553707 to St Lawrence 68-967043
From this Kent church with intervisibility to other sites, the ley passes through an earthwork at DARENTH WOOD before crossing the Thames. It slides along the edge of the churchyard at MUCKING, that gained it's ugly name from a Saxon tribe. This edging of the yard figures well because the grounds are artificially raised several feet above the surrounding landscape.

On this, once stood a pagan temple. The church itself contains a green man and a moon goddess carving. CORRINGHAM AND FOBBING CHURCHES are next, the latter displaying dragon carvings in the porch. RAYLEIGH MOUNT follows, a high site that plays host, together with the flanking church, to five more leys. A few further leys just miss the mount but it is possible that the entire hill crest, containing the church and castle mound, was an earthwork, so would have included the further leys. Three miles on the alignment reaches PLUMBEROW MOUNT tumulus, Hockley, that includes ley EX152. Over the river the ley covers a long stretch coming close to a few high land marks before finishing at ST LAWRENCE CHURCH where EX126n also terminates.

EX06 Grays 177-631793 to Pleshey 167-663143
This ley starts at the enigmatic subterranean DENE HOLES complex and runs to a low stone at BULPHAM CHURCH that has slight magnetic properties. It was once the base of a preaching cross according to Dr Rudge of the old 1950s Essex Field Club. Next comes MOUNTNESSING CHURCH, possessing a green man inside. Just prior to the church the ley passes through a deciduous wood, where, on the line, towers a lone Scots Pine, a tree noted by Watkins to have such marking tendencies. Further north the line arrives at BACONS FARM at Heybridge.

This site is interesting because Bacon is often a corruption of Beacon and so could be included on a ley. The farm has at lest two, may four leys through it, the major pair edging a moat as they frequently do at earth bank sites. The ley then goes to INGATESTONE CHURCH where a stone lays by the south wall. The ley then passes over the two stones that flank the Fryerning road junction in the main street. Whether this can be counted as a separate site is hard to say, rather depending if the numerous stones in this town were once all one stone or separate edifices. Before reaching the church the ley crosses a playing field once known as Stonefield.

A possible site a few miles north is Writtle Deer Park that was once called Stone Wood. We then arrive at a pub on the A1060 at BLACKWALL BRIDGE where leys EX100.5 and EX80s also cross at this three way meet marked by a small stone. The ley finally terminates at PLESHEY EARTH WORK where it strikes the bank at right angles rather than clipping the edge as is usual. But if the 'edge' rule is broken the ley invariably will end at the site as it does here. Also, the Pleshey complex stems from many eras with much alteration, so it is difficult to define the original perimeter.

EX30n Chipping Ongar 167-554031 to Wethersfield 167-712313

This ley starts at the Norman built mound. But it is considered to be of Saxon origin and thus could be older as is often the case. The ley follows the River Roding valley to a 'secondary' point of a moat at Marks Hall near Margaret Roding where another possible ley crosses. The consistency of halls and farms in Essex named after the Norman manor owner, Adelolf de Mark, on leys, may be worth noting. A choice of ancient sites may have been deliberate in the placing of his properties. HIGH EASTER CHURCH is next. The churchyard contains a stone through which EX102 also runs, from Wallbury Camp. LITTLE DUNMOW CHURCH is included next with it's dragons and animal carvings. Also here is a gravestone that may have been a converted mark stone.

A more definite stone is found at the next point at BARDFIELD SALING CHURCHYARD by the gate. A larger stone, some four feet across but worn very low, lies close by on the grass verge. Less than a mile off the ley finds another stone at a junction at NEW GREEN FARM. Finally we end the run at WETHERSFIELD where a stone, last used for horse mounting, now reposes just outside the churchyard by a house door.

For the ley hunter the following is a list of 30 ley lines that I have plotted in Essex. All have a minimum of 6 sites.

CB150	Foxton church to Elsenham church.
HF206	Standon stone to Great Waltham church.
KT65	Slade Green tumulus to Bowers Gifford church.
EX75n	Leper Stone to Ridgewell church.
EX114	Great Canfield mound to Asheldham Camp.
HF110	Broxbourne church to Sutton Camp.
EX82n	Coggeshall church to Great Bromley church.
EX125	West Hanningfield church to North Shoebury church.
EX03	Great Stambridge church to Easthorpe church.
EX102.5	Lucus Farm stones to Beacon Hill.
EX168	Lee's Priory to Wickford church.
EX95.5	Cressing Temple to St Osyth's Priory.
EX126s	Broomfield church to Shelford tumulus.
EX53	Wickham St Paul's church to Lady's Well, Suffolk.
EX109s	Toot Hill to Great Wakering church.
EX66	Little Waltham church to Colchester Castle.
EX87	Latton Priory to Goldhanger church.
EX144n	Bicknacre Priory to Southchurch church.
EX170n	Langford church to Prittlewell Priory.
EX93n	Theydon Priory to Burnham on Crouch church.
EX85	Castle Hedingham cross to Capel St Mary church, Suffolk.
EX102	Wallbury Camp to Hatfield Peveral Priory.
EX32	Clavering earthwork to Dullingham church, Suffolk.
EX126n	Faulkbourne church to St Lawrence church.
EX01.5	Lord's Walk earthwork to Wicken Bonham church.
EX73	Thresher's Bush stone to Copford church.
EX93n	Clavering church to Pitchbury earthwork.
EX23	Purfleet beacon hill to Ingatestone stones.
EX152	Little Leighs church to Plumberow Mount.
EX158	Clavering earthwork to Fyfield church.

Chapter Four

Essex site gazetteer

The following is a list of all verified and probable Neolithic and Bronze Age sites known to the author. Also included are all the parish churches with pagan carvings or features of interest that are considered worthy of a visit. The gazetteer cannot be considered to be completely exhaustive but I feel justified in claiming that it could be 90% or more so.

The author has visited almost every site mentioned. Information on the remainder was supplied by colleagues who were instrumental in initiating my research. In turn they were inspired by the late Dr E.A.Rudge who, with the Essex Field Club, did much pioneering work in the 1940s and 50s long before earth mysteries came into vogue. Some stones I located by dint of listing in the Essex Naturalist magazine of that period.

Interestingly, in Watkins book, *The Old Straight Track*, he mentions a correspondent from Chelmsford who states; 'This is a county with very ancient earthworks, innumerable moats, mark stones, stocks mounds, camps etc, and working on results in my own county has proved a perfect mine of discovery and verification.' This tends to lend validity to my assertion that Essex stones were placed there in ancient times.

A few stones and tumuli mentioned do not now exist, but I have mentioned them for the sake of completion and as an aid to ley hunters.

The gazetteer site headings consist of the usual place name or that of the nearest village followed by the Ordnance Survey Landranger map number and grid reference. Then I add code

Abbess Roding

letters for the type of structure/carving to be found at the site to enable the reader to tell at a glance what may be found there.

Glossary of heading code letters:

BH Beacon/Holy hill.
C Cursus.
CC Causeway Camp.
DH Dene Hole.
EW Earthwork.
GV Grove.
H Henge.

LL Ley lines prominently feature.
S Stone.
T Tumulus.
W Holy Well.
X Preaching cross.
Z Maze.

The following are church features in stone, wood and glass.

A Animal.
CA Church Architecture.
D Dragon.
E Exhibitionist.
G Gargoyles and grotesques.

GM Green Man.
MP Mouth Puller.
P Painting.
SC Solar Carving.
TP Tongue Poker.

Abbess Roding   167-572115 SC.

One of several of the Roding villages, the prefix, Abbess, is derived from the nuns of Barking Abbey who were patrons in the middle ages. St. Edmund's church possesses a square font with unusual carvings of stars, suns and moons. Astrological symbols were the result of foreign influence born of the 12th century crusades to the Holy Land. The fact that the Church allowed them into their buildings as well as the native pagan carvings demonstrates the fundamental difference in the Church of the time. This is no one-off font either. Both Little Laver and Fryerning churches have the same carvings. I have also found a six point 'hex' star at Little Sampford church, although they may not be directly related.

Alphamstone

If such symbols were acceptable when these churches were built then things had changed by 1638 when the Archdeacon ordered that those at Abbess Roding be covered in green paint to hide them. Paint traces still remain. An iron band around the font prevents it splitting apart. Cromwell's soldiers may have been the vandalising culprits.

Alphamstone   155-878354 LL. S.

In terms of stones in-situ St.Barnabus' church is the best in Essex. At least 11 are to be found in the churchyard which appears to be an artificial, raised platform. The church is also on a Bronze age burial mound, urns from which are in Colchester museum. The sarsen stones could be what is left of the uprights and capping stones of the chambered barrow, probably similar to Kits Coty House in Kent.

The largest stone lies adjacent to the west wall of the church and measures about 5 ft x 4 ft x 1 ft. Five slightly smaller stones line the henge at the west bank. Two more of undetermined size, that could weigh half a ton, are partly buried in the road bank flanking the entrance path. A two foot plus lump sits by the church's north-east corner and another is actually inside the building incorporated into the west wall.

There may be several further stones outside in front of the bricked up west door and south door but they are flush to the ground so it is difficult to assess them. Several blocks also grace village driveways, and a small example lies wedged into the road bank to the east at grid ref 881354 close to the village name sign.

These sarsens are not indigenous to Essex, meaning that they are either glacial erratics or were bought in from the west country. Alphamstone may be a contender for the site of a possible stone circle.

The church itself has little trace of carvings, but has an uncommon north door entrance. From Alphamstone, ley line

Arkesden

SF155 runs north to Great Henny church and on to Dedham church, Suffolk. EX59n passes through to Lamarsh and Boxford churches, and to Gosfield in the other direction.

Ardleigh 168-054297 A. D. G. GM. TP.

The porch of the parish church is amongst the most interesting in Essex. One carving is a wyvern; a two legged dragon with a knot in it's tail.

Above the spandrels of the inner door are sculptures described in one guide book as Adam and Eve. However, neither figure appears to be feminine, and what is more, they are reminiscent of dryads or woodwoses; male spirits of the forest. Each stands in a welter of foliage as evidence.

Two chess-piece like statues surmount the porch buttress pillars. Both are hoofed and similar to a horse. But the head of one has too short a muzzle and the other has a long neck and a face like a lion or a dog. It also appears to be sitting on a throne.

Inside are some tiny dragon carvings on the rood screen and some Victorian floor tiles have perpetuated the pagan theme - most likely unwittingly - by their design of tongue poking heads and immersing leaves.

Arkesden 154-482346 D. G. S.

St. Margaret's church has gargoyles high on it's tower. One of these is a wyvern with it's tail curled beneath it and a head that departs from the norm by bearing somewhat human features. Incorporated into the churchyard wall is a stone about 28 inches across.

The village itself is abundant with stones of which some must be of an ancient placing. The large puddingstone memorial in the churchyard is not, and four stones at the eastern end of the village at ref 484343 have almost certainly been moved because a stream and a bridge are to be found inside their square patterned placing. However, they do mark the meeting of three ways and a ley line. The largest is 34 inches high and the smallest about 2 feet tall. Moving through the village to the central pub we find a pudding stone by the pavement at grid reference 483344 measuring about 2 ft x 2 ft x 18".

Closer to the church by another stream bridge is a further boulder of the same sandstone as the four at the eastern bridge of approximately the same size.

Puddingstone is a conglomerate where sandstone is dotted with silica of flint pebbles. It is also called mother stone or bleeding stone, the latter due to the fact that the pebbles eventually fall out due to wear. The whole looks distinguishingly pretty in the sunshine after a shower.

Ashdon 154-593409 S.
A stone graces the grass verge near this village outside a bungalow called Midsummer Hill. It is 2.5 feet high and is near a farm called Goldstones. Watkins found that some leys have sites in their path with the word, 'gold' in the place name that had some connection with a midsummer sunrise alignment. Here we find two names that may lend a clue to ancient practices. Other interesting 'gold' names are found at Golden Cross, Goldhanger, Goldsticks Farm and Goldens Farm near Panfield.

Asheldham 168-972012 EW. LL.
There are actually two earthworks at Asheldham but the larger is very difficult to trace. It covers an oval area of 16 acres and encloses a pond, a hall and the parish church of St. Lawrence. The smaller is much more definable and is wedged within the curve of the north side road, covering 6 acres. Its southern bank and ditch are visible, and it is marked on the map as a settlement. Both sites are considered to be pre-Roman.

Three leys hit this site, two running north-east with one of these through the centre which is unusual. However, the old one inch ordnance maps show a raised area at this point that might well mean that this was the original structure and that the bank and ditch came later. The third ley comes in from Beeleigh tumulus and Little Waltham church, ending at this earthwork.

Ashingdon   178-869960 LL. (X).

Nothing now remains of the preaching cross that once stood where three roads meet that is still called Golden Cross. It is added to the gazetteer for completion. The area was so named in the middle ages after Gilbert de Goldhord who in turn is supposed to have derived his name from a hoard of treasure found here. However, nothing is said of where the treasure went or if it was actually dug up, etc, and it seems odd that the cross should gain the man's name, and why should somebody name themselves after a treasure find?

As crosses were often Christianised standing stones it may have more to do with the word 'gold' where there are frequent connections with solar alignment and midsummers day. Goldhanger church and the stone at Goldstones farm appear to have this kind of inference.

At Golden Cross two leys cross, one running to the Venus Stone at Hawkwell, EX79n, while a summer solstice alignment points us to Beacon Hill on which Canewdon church stands. The latter site could have been a sighting marker similar to those found at stone circles.

If in the area, it is worth a visit to Ashingdon church up on St. Michael's Hill which overlooks the site of King Cnut's Battle of Ashingdon, from which ghostly moans of the dead are still claimed to be heard.

Audley End   154-523388 S.

Opposite the entrance to the stately home that is on the site of a Benedictine abbey, is a large sandstone block some 4 ft x 3 ft. It is thought that it was moved from it's original location. This stone demonstrates the strange importance given to such megaliths in that the council fence erecters deemed to build around the stone rather than move it or break it up.

Aythorpe Roding   167-585137 S.

Four stones rest on the grass verge outside Lucus Farm consisting of two types of stone. One has stood for at least as long as the farm house whilst the others were unearthed by the plough in the mid seventies. None of them may have any significance but the spot from where one was retrieved is on a ley line. It is possible that the stones were once buried during the days of the 'stone killing' purges. The name Lucus, which is not the current owners name, but stems back to 1805 as shown on the first edition O/S map, is Latin for grove so could just possibly refer to an oak grove that druids would have used, who in turn might have adopted a sacred stone age venue. The root of the word also refers to light, as in Lucifer, the archetypal devil, meaning shining one. This could have bearings on solar alignments. This root is also found in Lucus Lane in Castle Hedingham where a number of stones decorate the streets.

Bardfield Saling   167-686266 G. LL. S.

The church of SS Peter and Paul has some gargoyles but the main feature is its two stones close to the churchyard gate. One inside the yard is of a reddish calcite of a maximum of 21 inches across by 8 inches thick. Outside on the wide grass verge is a sarsen example of some 4 feet across and almost circular. Part underground, it stands 18 inches high with the appearance of being well worn by centuries of weathering.

Three leys meet here, and it is notable that the closest sites of Lindsell, New Green Farm and Goldsticks Farm all contain a stone. The trio of leys then link another five stones farther out. Stones, as mentioned in the previous chapter, are probably the heart of the ley system and thus would go further towards confirming a ley's existence than would a church minus such an addition.

New Green Farm 167-690275 S.
At the entrance to this farm where three ways meet is one of the above mentioned stones. It is 18 inches high by 1 foot in diameter. A young lady equestrian told me that, 'possessing a psychic sensibility' she found the farm a particularly 'tranquil' area. This ties in fairly well with theories that stones, in accord to healing property notions of folk legend, would be beneficial to humans.

Basildon 178-714898 A.
Holy Cross church boasts two carvings in the spandrels of the wooden porch. One is a dragon with an arrow head tongue and a looping tail. It is crocodile like in style. Opposite is an animal usually described as a bear, standing on or climbing up a branch or ragged staff sprouting a flower of six segments. It has a collar such as once worn by tame bears but it's overall shape and its lower tusks suggest that it is a wild boar. The animal may or may not have any symbolic significance.

Beauchamp Roding 167-578098 A. S.
The 14th century church of St. Botolph is mainly known for its stone legend which echoes other such stories across the land. The church of Clowne in Derbyshire, to name one. The stone, which was restood a few years ago during a 'secret raid' by an earth mysteries group, stands 3 ft 6" high by 4 ft long.

Legend tells that when the villagers decided to build a church they opted to utilise a large stone for material that stood a quarter of a mile away upon a hill crest. They dragged the stone down the hill one evening and left it ready for the morning. But next day they found that the stone, to their astonishment, had returned to the top of the hill! So they dragged it down again, to find, next morning, it had mysteriously returned to its old resting place. A third attempt was made, but again it was found on top of the hill. The Church now considered this to be an omen, and that the devil must have moved the old stone. As a result the church was built on the hill and the stone remained unmolested.

Basildon

Variations on the theme often have the church itself move across a road, but the devil is usually cited as the culprit. Sometimes he is enormous and with wings so he lifts the church and flies to the chosen spot. These legends clearly indicate that great reverence was placed on such stones, and that the hill or alternative location was a sacred pagan site. The Beauchamp tale may be a garbled and fanciful version of an argument between the church hierarchy and the pagan builders as to the most suitable spot for a holy building. The Church would desire a convenient place and the villagers the long established holy hill top.

Inside the church we find a carving of a pig's head in the act of tongue poking. It is on the north wall of the chancel and painted white. Both the pig and protruding tongue are fertility symbols although why animals are shown in a human act is not known. It tends to negate the theory that tongue pokers depict hanged men, unless they had a habit of hanging pigs in days of old! The pig features in Celtic mythology and could represent the sow goddess Ceridwen.

Bedlars Green   167-533204 EW.
Known as Portingbury Hills, this is a very indistinct site which is hard to date. It is situated in Hatfield Forest near Stansted airport and marked on the ordnance map.

Billericay   178-689953 T.
A large earthen bank can be found in Norsey Woods called the Deerbank but is is not likely to be of great antiquity. The tumulus that stands at the edge of the trees is, however, considered to be Bronze age or Neolithic. it is 5 feet high by 45 feet across. it was opened in 1865 and contained three British urns, ashes and bones. Another barrow stood up until 1989 on the north side of the wood at reference 684957 but alas it is now under a garage. It was 5 feet high 50 ft across and 7 urns were found in it. Two leys run through the remaining tumulus.

Blackmore   167-603017 GM. S.
St.Lawrence church served the now defunct Jerico Priory that was frequented by King Henry VIII. To the left of the porch of the Norman church lies a small 18 inch stone hinting that the site is of greater antiquity. A green man can be seen inside on a roof boss.

Blackwall Bridge   167-680083 LL. S.
This 18 inch high stone is precisely where I expected to find one in accord with Alfred Watkins' ley hunting criteria. The ley is EX06 - described in the previous chapter - coming up from the Grays dene holes via the stone at Bulpham church. It then crosses the A1060 Chelmsford road where the Roxwell road meets it to form a three way meet.

The stone rests by the side gate of a pub, and two more leys pass through the spot, on coming from the Beauchamp Roding stone and Roxwell church on its way to the cursus at Springfield. The other goes to the Willingale stone and Wickham Bishops church. As this pub is called the Horse and Groom then the stone may have been used as a mounting block.

Bocking   167-758258 G. TP.
The large church of St. Mary has a low frieze of gargoyles and a tongue poker on its south side wall (the tower to your left). It has long curling hair that gives it an animal appearance, with bold eyebrows and a wide mouth. The tongue is of normal length and pokes slightly out.

Bowers Gifford   178-756873 D.
Flanking the east window of this picturesque little 15th century church of St. Margaret are two cute looking dragons curled like snoozing cats. St. Margaret is a dragon slayer but these pair are unmolested and seem far from the threatening creature they are supposed to be in Britain.

Boxted 168-998333 G. S.
Acting as a foundation, a stone juts out from the wall on the south west corner of the Norman church of St.Peter. It measures 3 feet by 18 inches and is of a reddish hue, not limestone. The church also has some tower mounted gargoyles.

Bradwell-on-Sea 168-004069 G. TP.
St.Thomas's church has a row of small stone heads on the south wall including some grotesques and a tongue poker. Inside, the font has a human head carved into each of its four sides. But as is so often the case with pagan carvings, one of them is poking out its tongue! These pagan sculptures seldom come as a matching pair or as a complete line of them. One is given the impression that the masons would 'slip one in on the quiet' to get the pagan oar in so to speak.

St.Peters Church 168-031082 S.
On the site of the Roman fort of Othona this Saxon building was built by St. Cedd in the mid 7th century making it one of the oldest used churches in England. Until 1920 it was used as a barn. Inside is a small stone measuring 15 inches across. It may have no relevance although two leys end here where a pagan temple it is thought may have stood.

Braintree 167-756230 D. S.
St. Michael's church has Norman foundations and a St. Michael and a dragon carving on a boss in the chapel. Outside, a stone pokes proud of the wall base at the north east corner measuring 2 feet in length.

Broomfield 167-705105 S.
St. Leonard's church has one of the six round towers in Essex and was possibly started by the Saxons. A sarsen stone juts out of the south wall about 18 inches.

Bulmer

Bulmer 155-843402 GM.
St. Andrew's church has a white, 15th century font with a fine example of a green man engraving, considered one of the best in England of its period. It has foliage of grape vines sprouting from its forehead and mouth. A pagan temple is thought to have occupied this site. A modern tapestry map of the area can be found here that the author, seeking earth mysteries, found very useful as it resulted in finding a ley and a twin stone site. It names a small wood near Wickham St Paul as the Grove and a field south of Bulmer Tye as Golden Ley. A ley was then found to extend from this wood through Nether House Farm stones to the Golden Ley stones and on to Middleton church.

Bulmer Tye 155-850376 LL. S.
On the grass verge and on the drive to a vet's surgery next to Gentry's Farm off the A131 are two stones some 2 feet across. Both have laid there for some time and may not simply be unearthed by the plough. The field on the north side is called Golden Ley. The root word gold often links with some kind of solar alignment, and stones are nearly always present. Three leys cross here, one running through the said field. Another, EX45, might commence at a grove; the wood into which the ley intrudes is called the grove. It also includes another stone at Nether House Farm, and four churches. The second ley includes the stone where three ways meet at Audley End. The third ley includes the stone at Ridgewell and those at Gestingthorpe.

Bulpham 177-637859 LL. S.
Here at St. Mary's church a small block of limestone about 18 inches across and only 9 inches high protrudes from the ground besides the lychgate inside the churchyard. It was last used for horse mounting when the vicar arrived by equine transport. Dr E.A. Rudge lists the stone as the probable base of a preaching cross. It displays a magnetic quality by deflecting a magnetic compass by up to 8 degrees. So far I think it might be tied in to lunar phases as has been found elsewhere.

Ley line EX06 takes in this stone from the Dene Holes to include two more stones to the north. Another ley, EX79s comes in from the well at North Ockenden and then goes on to four more churches to Great Stambridge.

Burnham on Crouch   168-949970 G.

St. Mary's church has a few well defined grotesques on its porch with heavy eyebrows, short triple horns and round, gaping mouths.

Canewdon   178-896946 BH. G.

The 15th century church of St.Nicholas is steeped in history. Built on a Saxon site, the Danish army of King Cnut camped on the hill before defeating Edmund Ironside in 1016. Cnut is said to have built three churches after the victory; Ashingdon, after which the battle was named, Hockley and Canewdon. However, this village is mistakenly said to have been named after him, in fact the place was originally Carenduna, a Saxon word meaning hill of Cana's people, who also dwelt on nearby Canvey Island. 400 years ago the prominent height was used as a beacon sighting hill.

The church has a long association with pagan beliefs and practices. As long as the tower stands the village is reputed to have six witches. Another story refers to nine witches of which one will die if a stone falls from the tower. Walk around the church in a widdershins (anti-clockwise) direction on Samhain/Hallowe'en three times and the devil is supposed to appear.

In 1989 an acquaintance of mine tried this in a hired aircraft because the police close off the site at Halloween. Having circled the prescribed amount of times the aircraft's alternator malfunctioned and all but the essential electrical systems were turned off as they made a dash back for the airport! But as soon as they were clear of Canewdon it came back on again! Make of that what you will.

George Pickingill, a reputed master of witches with a long pedigree of east anglian witches, lived here in a cottage next to the Anchor pub and was buried in unconsecrated ground in 1909. He was raised by gypsies and is said to have been one of the foremost authorities on the craft in the land. It is also said that if he stood outside his cottage and whistled all the village's nine witches would appear.

On the church's outer walls we find a few battered grotesque heads. The most discernible one is a man/beast with round ears and short horns. Inside are the remnants of several human and animal head carvings but they are almost unrecognisable. Some are described as a woman, a bird and a beast. Their mutilation occurred only last century when a well dressed gentleman marched into the building armed with a hammer and chisel. With these he proceeded to attack the carvings before marching out again. The vicar remonstrated with him and the man claimed to have been commissioned to do the dirty deed. He then managed to escape, evading arrest, and was never seen again!

Psychics and ordinary mortals alike claim that the building is alive with different 'energies'. Considering the local history and the many ghosts of white ladies, coach and horses, crusader and a black dog, this may not be surprising. Odd noises are often heard there. Sounds like the scraping of a brick on the floor have been heard.

Enter an area by the tower sometimes and all seems to go unnaturally quiet, as if it was a 'dead' spot. The church is also on two ley lines.

Castle Hedingham 155-788358 EW.
The Norman castle here sits atop a natural knoll surrounded by ramparts enclosing some three acres. The earthwork entertains a couple of ley lines and could well be pre-Norman.

Catmere End

St. Nicholas's Church 155-785355 A. S. TP. X.

This churchyard can boast the only remaining preaching cross in Essex. It survived because up to 70 years ago it propped up the cellar roof of the Falcon Inn pub in the village. It now serves as a war memorial. It has heart shaped ribbon and flower work of the 13th century.

One of the few carvings on the outside of the church is a strange tongue poker with a fairly conventional if wide head but with legs sprouting from its ears! They start from just above the knees and bend down to the side of the head. It is the only example I have discovered in Essex, or anywhere else as yet, although the type is known as a nobody. The meaning, if any, is lost. Inside are more carvings of men and animals.

One of the tiny lanes to the east of the church is called Luces Lane. This name may have stemmed from the latin root meaning light, as found at Lucus Farm, Aylthorpe Roding. If so then it might have connections with solar alignments as is often the case. To back the theory are three stones lurking on the lane corners, one up against the road sign. They measure 3 ft x 2 ft, 2 ft x 1 ft and 18" X 1 ft. They could have been standing stones or perhaps the broken base of the cross.

Catmere End 154-497388 S.

At a lonely cross road, lost in the long grass lies a stone of limestone content. Many years ago it stood proudly upright. My source of information was an elderly lady from the Essex UFO Research Group who directed me to it, she and her fellow school children would sit on it whilst waiting for the bus. It is a fair size for Essex measuring 5 ft 9" x 3 ft 9" and thus must weigh upwards of a ton.

Chadwell St Mary 177-645785 S.

Laying close to the east wall of St. Mary's church is a sarsen stone about 2 ft 6" by 2 ft. The date 1621 is inscribed on it but it could have occupied the spot for a lot longer than that.

Chalkwell 178-859862 (T).
This one time barrow in Chalkwell park, Southend is mentioned for completion. According to 19th century historian, Philip Benton, it still existed in 1886 when it was still 4 feet high. He located it in the north-east corner of Fishponds Field to the east of the hall. It was Celtic and contained bones, coins and a chain. Southend museum staff actually doubt Benton's claims, and this seems typical of the attitude to 'outsiders' that historical authorities have.

When the owner of the Venus Stone at Hawkwell informed them of his find he was told that it was just a lump of rock, yet it is undoubtedly, by the criterium used on other stones, of ancient placing. Nor do they seem aware of the stone in Eastwood church or have any mention in the local museum of the 8 acre Sutton Camp that should have protection orders on them. This underlines the need for an interest in earth mysteries if only so as to cause people to become aware of this aspect of our heritage. These are some of the oldest man-made artifacts in the world yet are in danger of disappearing forever due to official and public ignorance.

Chignall Smealy 167-668118 S.
The all brick church here is unadorned but on the grass verge by the road is a small stone a fraction over a foot round. It appears to deflect a magnetic compass by a few degrees in a similar manner to the Bulpham Stone. A short way along the road where three ways meet is a further stone about 18" x 18" but displays no odd effects. The church is thought to be on a pagan temple site, and several leys pass over it.

Chipping Ongar 167-554031 EW. LL.
The Norman keep here is typically thought to be a modification of an earlier work. The three leys I have found here all skirt the edge in the usual manner. Part of the outer bailey rampart appears to have once encircled a large area used as a defensive settlement by the Anglo-Saxons.

St. Martin's Church 167-553030 MP. TP.
This 11th century building has a fine mouth pulling grotesque inside and a small addition outside together with a tongue poker.

Church End 167-733273 S.
Goldsticks Farm is on the Braintree Road beside the River Pant, it has a stone lying by a barn 2 ft 6" high. The root name gold may lend it some significance. A ley runs to it from the stones at Bardfield Saling church and goes on to stones at Stonebridge Hill and Wakes Colne Green. Just to the north of the farm where three ways meet is a cottage at 733274 with several small stones out front.

Clavering 167-471319 EW. G.
Just north of the church is an earthwork called The Castle. This is a typical misnomer as no castle remains here today, if eve. No traces are visible in the flat 300 ft x 185 ft interior or rough meadow grass. The east-end moat has become filled, so allowing easy access, and the remaining ditch is about 15 feet deep and over 30 feet across and strewn with trees and bush. Three leys that skirt the ditch may indicate that the site is pre-Norman. The church of SS Mary and Clement has a few small gargoyles and grotesques inside and out.

Coggeshall 168-853230 A. CA. GM.
The large church of St. Peter has an outer frieze of gargoyles which include animals such as a ram, bull and what looks like a monkey. Inside, at the chancel end, are at least three green men on roof bosses. Also here is an interesting modern statue of, presumably, St Mary, it is made from a light coloured wood and near life size. It, however, has an odd pagan like ambience, resembling a wood elemental or a fusion of a tree and a woman, with a serene expression and long golden hair.

Colchester

Colchester 168-001253 G.

St. James church stands on East Hill. The tower top has four gargoyles of which one is a copy of the original that tumbled down in the 1884 earthquake. They are like strange birds with tall, pointed ears and a deep set beak.

St. Leonard's Church 168-012248 G. P. TP.

On a busy street at the east end of the town this church served the dock area but is now disused, if maintained. Access is restricted but visible on the porch is a grotesque head. Traces of paintings can be seen over the nave arch inside. Two tongue pokers are also visible inside in high positions. The tower has 'gargoyles' but in the form of the four evangelist symbols/Christian esoteric signs for the elements, the angel, lion, bull and eagle that correspond to Aquarius, Leo, Taurus and Scorpio, or air, fire, earth and water.

Colchester Castle 168-999253 E. EW.

The town's Norman castle was built on a Temple to Mithras a Persian imported deity. It gave way to an English stone castle that stands today as Colchester's main museum primarily dedicated to the area's prolific Roman remains. The castle site could be much older than is known.

The museum is worth a visit, because upstairs, almost ignored in a window bay is a very rare pagan carving, a sheela-na-gig, languishing with other salvaged carvings from unknown churches. This is a female figure in a sitting position holding open her genitals! It is probably a fertility symbol and evident that the carvers looked upon sexuality with different eyes than we do today. This is the sole example in Essex and came from Easthorpe church near Marks Tay. She is typically crudely designed with large, bear-like ears and no breasts. The genital area is also grossly enlarged. The slab on which she is carved bears three letters that resemble. EMM. However, the final two letters are more like Saxon runes for the letter M and D. I have no idea as to what they actually are.

Copford

Three stone heads accompany the main feature. One is like the Roman goddess Minerva or the Greek Artemis. Another may be a female tongue poker. The third is a bust of a flat faced man with a hood, with his arms in a praying position.

Colne Engaine 168-850304 D. S.

St. Andrew's church was started by the Normans and has two stones in the nave wall on the north and south sides. Inside is a tall wooden candlestick holder of some size with a carving of a dragon spiralling around it. its legless and wingless style make it what is known as a guivre.

Copford 168-935228 D. P.

St. Michael's church has the finest example in Essex and many other counties of remaining original wall paintings, lending us a good idea of what the interior of most medieval churches looked like. These were discovered in 1884 when the whitewash was removed. The paint was applied in about 1150, and mainly depicts geometric patterns, biblical scenes and angels. Some of the colours were enhanced shortly after their discovery. The apsidal nave's arch is resplendent with 12 circular signs of the zodiac from Aquarius to Capricorn with a semi-circular symbol for the sun at one end and the moon at the other. The Church obviously did not frown upon the 'occult' art of astrology in the 12th century as it did in the mid 17th when it was banned, and when the paint work was probably covered.

What is odd about the signs is that they do not begin at Aries and and at Pisces as they should. Each sign also has a different number of 'stars' in it, and with varying numbers of points on them that may signify something or not.

A wooden statue is to be found here on the pulpit railings of St George slaying a dragon. He has lost his spear so the dragon could be said to be winning the tussle - a sign of the times?

Copthall Green 167-424016 LL. S.
A stone lies flat on the grass by a bend in a track in front of a country house. It is sandstone and measures 5ft 6" x 3ft making it one of the largest in Essex. Three leys visit this stone that include in their path Ambresbury Banks and Upshire church, close by, and Latton Priory and the Hobbs Cross stone farther out. I was notified of this stone by John Ruse then discovered that I already had the crossing leys on the map. So I could have literally found the stone by simply visiting the cross ley site in a similar manner to when I first went to Blackwall Bridge.

Danbury 167-779051 EW.
This hilltop earthwork, situated just below the church of St John is of a Danish design as the name infers. But being as two leys skirt it the six acre enclosure may be older. The rampart encloses a graveyard with the southern rim being the most distinct at six feet high and probably one of the most picturesque in the land being as it is mostly decorated with garden plants, lending a colourful border when in bloom.

A local legend states that the devil once visited the church and as a result the roof was blown off. He later returned and stole the bell and, apparently able to fly, dropped it on nearby Bell Wood Hill where a 25 foot crater still exists. It is said that no ringer would then toll the new bell!

Dedham 168-048332 G. S.
The huge church of St. Mary's close to the River Stour reflects that the little village was once a prosperous wool trading centre. The church has a number of gargoyles, some with three short horns, a common feature elsewhere, too.

Two stones can be found here, one to the left of the north side porch which is the larger of the two measuring 2 ft x 2 ft 6" x 2 ft. The other lies on the south side and is used as a memorial with Edward and Martha Ward inscribed on it.

Dengie 168-989016 A. G.
The small church of St. James has three carvings on the outer tower wall. Two are lions and the other is a gargoyle incorporating both lion and human features.

Doddinghurst 167-589999 GM.
Inside All Saints church is a green man on the octagonal font. Each side has the same four petal flower like design but only one has a foliate man in its centre. This singular lay out is typical of church carvings and is also found on the font at Bradwell on Sea.

Eastwood 178-869889 D. S.
St. Lawrence's church by Southend airport's runway has traces of Norman work and a stone that lends the site great antiquity. Roughly circular, about 18 inches across, it actually juts up about three inches through the floor boards between the pews. Few churches have them in such an obtrusive location, they are usually wedged into a wall such as at Alphamstone. On the adjacent pillar is evidence of its pagan origins in the form of some medieval graffiti engravings. Crudely done, they depict a St George type figure armed with a spear. Below is a winged dragon with worm- like characteristics.

The local clergy and parishioners usually, rather amusingly, like to refer to the dragon as a boat! That, or try to steer you off the subject. This attitude is reminiscent of the reaction to the sheela na gig in Melbourne, Derbyshire, which is called a 'grinning cat' in the brochure. On one visit to Eastwood I was given an enthusiastic, voluntary tour of the church by a boy scout. I then led him to the stone with the inference that it was the oldest item in their itinerary, with the hope that, young as he was, he might have been told something of it. At this he adopted an expression something akin to mild horror and proceeded to make a hasty retreat in the direction of the tower, never to show his face again!

Elmdon

Three leys run through the site. Eastwood may have connections with the mysterious warrior monks of the middle ages, the Knights Templar, their name derived from the Temple of Solomon in Jerusalem. Between 1280 and 1303 the Templars owned nearly 100 acres of land in the area. Temple Farm, 1.5 miles from the church was a preceptory of theirs, and the church is orientated towards the farm.

Three saints, Catherine, Christopher and Lawrence were adopted by the order. St. Lawrence's church has a ground plan based on a gridiron on which the saint was martyred in the 3rd century. He claimed to be the guardian of treasure but would not reveal its whereabouts or precise nature other than it was the beggars and cripples amongst the people. Being as the Templars are now considered to have been custodians of some kind of secret knowledge, ie a treasure, it is not difficult to see why they identified with such a man.

Elmdon 154-462398 G. T.

St. Nicholas's church has some tower gargoyles. At a lower level on the south wall are some further examples resembling devils. One has two horns and bulging eyes, another is similar but has enlarged eyebrows and pointed ears rather than horns. Behind the church on a hill is Elmdonbury, a large tumulus, any details of which I have yet to learn.

Epping 167-439004 EW.

Epping forest is now the largest remaining tract of the old Waltham forest. At the northern end, close to the main road, is Ambresbury Banks. This earthwork covers 12 acres and was last used, it is speculated, by the Iceni Queen Boudicca in her final stand against the Roman legions. However, a number of other earthworks also make this claim. It is 600 yards around with 6 foot ramparts, and a ditch averaging 15 feet across.

Originally the bank and ditch were at least 10 feet high and deep. Pottery finds from the Bronze age show that it was not built during the Roman period. As with many of these earth constructions there is little evidence of occupation on a permanent basis.

A ley commences from the east side and another runs along the southern edge making for the Copthall Green Stone, and Broxbourne church in the Herts direction.

Epping Upland 167-443045 S.

Originally Norman, All Saints was the parish church for Epping. Under the south west buttress are lodged two small stones that may be of a pagan origin. Two leys commence at the church, and Dr Rudge listed several fragments of stone in the church grounds.

Feering 167-872204 TP.

The church of All Saints has an outside carving of a fine tongue poking lion. The lion is one of the Christian four holy animals and in conventional form not likely to be pagan. This lion seems a curious embellishment unless the masons used any type of animal for displaying this act.

Felstead 167-677204 D. G. S.

Holy Cross church has a Norman tower and several gargoyles along the gutters. Until recently, at the western end stood a stone of about 18 inches high lying by a low wall. It may have been moved to somewhere in the churchyard. The church leaflet says that it probably stood in the village a short distance away; this would be where three roads meet. It is interesting to note that when these stones are moved, it is felt, even in this century, that they subsequently belong in the churchyard. A similar event took place at Mount Bures. On a building by the main road junction in the village is an inscription on the gutter frieze proclaiming; 'George Boot made this house', with the date of 1596. The frieze is also decorated with leaves and green dragons.

Jutting proud as part of the corner bracket is a three foot wooden statue of the 'Hag of Felstead'. She is a strange, near naked lady similar to a ship's figurehead and may well have served the same purpose as a kind of guardian to fend off evil spirits. She is actually wearing a black harness affair that some consider may be a chastity belt! But her most intriguing features are her cloven feet and legs of a goat below the knee!

Nothing seems to be known about this woman that reminds one of a female version of the Greek god Pan. It might have been a caricature of a village resident considered to be a witch because the Pan figure became symbolic of the devil. Magazine researcher Ian Dawson, says that some locals think it is George Boot's wife who was the victim of a witches curse so he married her out of pity. He also says that many locals won't go near her, and say she is evil and even cross the road to avoid her! She may also be a fairy known as a glaistig, that dwelt in the nearby lake.

Whatever, one thing that I feel is extraordinary is that after all these years she is undamaged, no puritan purge has torn her down, no prudish Victorian has 'clothed' her with paint and no staggering drunk has aimed a bear bottle at her nose. Long may she watch over all who stroll pass beneath her!

Finchingfield   167-686328 A. D. G. GM. TP.

St. Andrew's church stands atop a hill in what is called the prettiest village in England. But visitors know little of its less pleasant past. Peddar's Cottage in Howe Street was a school in the 17th century run by a woman called Goofy Mumford. She would keep the girls behind after classes and teach them pagan crafts and spell making. She was later stoned and buried at a crossroad, a traditional resting place for witches. Two witch sticks carved with animals and fertility symbols were found in the cottage walls this century.

The church has grotesques inside including a tongue poking lion on the rood screen, dividing the chancel and the nave. There is also a green man and dragons that look like Godzilla! Solar

Foxearth

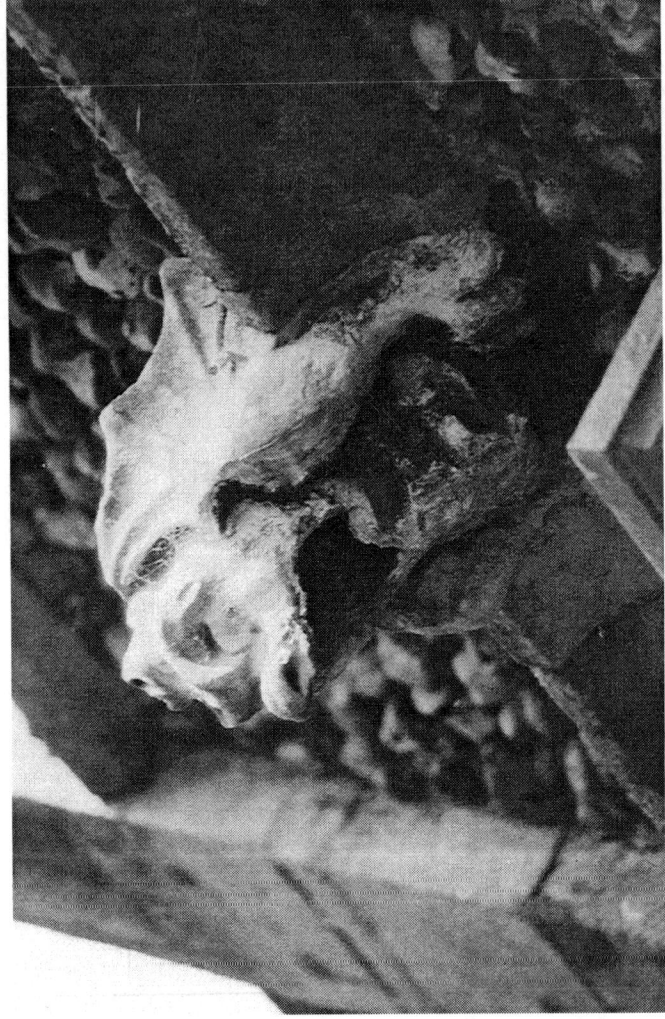

symbols can be found on a door. The stone work on the west door of the Norman tower has an uncommon depiction of a goat sandwiched tightly between two human heads. It has a long nose and a rounded beard.

Village Green   167-685329 S.
By the roadside north of the green is a stone, recumbent by a wall measuring 2 foot by almost a yard long.

Fingringhoe   168-030204 D.
St. Andrew's church has a carving of St Michael and the dragon on the porch spandrels. The beast is of the two legged wyvern variant with a curling tail.

Fobbing   178-718839 D.
Overlooking the Thames, St. Michael's church is on high ground typical of churches of that nomination. Carved into the porch woodwork is a crowned head reminiscent of the Roman god Poseidon or the Welsh Manawyddan, although neither of these are associated with wyverns, one of which is carved next to the head. The latter's main feature is that its jaws are being held open by a kneeling man wearing a hat. This is similar to the strength card in tarot packs. The creature may represent a sea dragon or the elemental power of the sea. The site is known to be pre-Saxon.

Foxearth   155-831448 G. TP.
SS Peter and Paul's church has suffered from restoration such as having a new tower. But inside are the remains of wall paintings and 3 tongue pokers on beam ends. On the outer north wall are some gargoyles, one with an upturned nose, animal forelegs and shoulder blade wings.

Fryerning 167-641016 EW.
Moore's Ditch is in the woods a mile north of the village. All that remains is a single straight bank and a 10 foot ditch of some 700 feet in length. But I know nothing of its history.

Gestingthorpe 155-812388 LL. S.
At the cross roads in this leafy village are two stones about 3 ft by 2 ft and 2 ft 6" high. 9 more fragments litter a garden, 3 in a field, 2 by a farm gate and two more by the church further south. The largest were last used as mounting blocks.

Legend says that the tallest turns around at midnight; a typical theme found all over the country where stones turn or dance and also drink once a night. The stones here also entertain two ley lines. Several stones came from a wood a little way off to the east that straddles one of these leys as it heads for the stones at Bulmer Tye.

Goldhanger 168-905089 D. LL.
St. Peter's church stands in a quiet village overlooking the River Blackwater, and is a fine example of medieval 'perpendicular' style construction. When Dave Hobbs and I first dropped by it was merely to 'tick' the place off my list and to get out of the rain. No hint is given in the guide books as to what is hidden within, and nobody we knew had reported anything of interest, so we were pleasantly surprised.

Six dragons are positioned in such a manner as to appear to have been deliberately tucked out of direct view. If you are tall (and Dave is) and possess keen eye sight you will be able to pick out a carving on a pillar at the junction of the chancel and the nave. An angel and a man are emerging from a forest. Look closer and note that a tiny dragon of only a few inches long is crawling out with them, or lurking on the edges. I think this is symbolic of man being led from the woods/wilderness ie, evil, where dragons dwell, with the angel as the salvationist. Typically this engraving is not matched on the opposite pillar.

Cross over the chancel to the bench end opposite and peer into the gloom at a circular dragon carved into the wood. Venture outside, and at head height flanking the 15th century porch doors are four balls of typical foliage in stone. But closer inspection of their upper and outer surfaces will reveal a small, 6 inch, lizard-like dragon on each as if purposely placed out of general sight. Two of them are fructifying beasts with their tails turning into large, three petal leaves.

More conventional is a stained glass window inside, although the detail of which is not easy to detect unless you push close between narrow set pews. It is a depiction of St. John the Evangelist portrayed as usual with a golden chalice with a beautifully fearsome dragon emerging from it in accord to his legend of nearly being poisoned when drinking. It might be interesting to learn why St.Peter is not shown here and if the glass designer knew of the other dragons about him. Many of the church staff and parishioners are completely oblivious to their existence.

The origin of the name Goldhanger, may refer to solar alignments as the term can do elsewhere. Hanger means hill, but there is not one, and gold is guessed to refer to yellow flowers in the vicinity. If it does refer to an alignment or sun worship then it is usually the summer solstice of June 24th, midsummer's day. St. John's day is June 24th! Is this only a coincidence?

I have previously mentioned the probability of terrestrial energies at Canewdon church. The ley here, EX03, originates at Great Stambridge church, also with peculiar energies, and the line runs on from Canewdon up to Lawing Chapel and Goldhanger, Tiptree earthwork and Easthorpe church. Two more leys also visit Goldhanger church.

Grays   177-631793 DH.
In Hangman's Wood are to be found vertical shafts some 70 feet deep and 8 feet wide that sink to the sub-terranean chalk level. Below we find a complicated network of tunnels and galleries.

The layout somewhat resembles a bunch of flowers as each shaft is surrounded by a cluster of 6 womb shaped chambers about 20 to 3o feet long and 15 feet high. Most clusters are connected by low tunnels to one or two others dug to gain access since they were first excavated in 1884-87. The whole interlinking complex covers about 4 acres. Unfortunately the shafts are fenced and locked, and climbing equipment is needed to get down there, as used when myself and a climbing club did it in 1995. Things were a little easier in 1968 when I first explored them, using a rope ladder and a rope tied to the back of a car! And they are dangerous, I was knocked unconscious by a falling lump of flint! I understand that another group goes down there on Sundays to study the flora and fauna especially the bats.

Of an unknown age, the name is derived from Dane because one rather poor theory was that the local villagers hid their valuables down there during Viking raids, or that the Danes themselves stored loot down there. If so, booty must have been of enormous proportions. The chalk mine theory does not fit either, because only a mile away chalk is readily available near the surface. In the 18th century a company was formed to explore them on the premise that it was the lost gold mine of the Roman King Cumobeline.

Found only in a few counties and thought Celtic, they are one of Britain's great ancient mysteries. As with Silbury Hill and Avebury it is difficult to fathom why so much effort went into gaining such an apparently un-cost effective return.

Most of the 50 odd shafts have been filled with soil and rubbish and most of the chamber clusters are reached via two shafts and subsequent tunnels; about 12 clusters remain. I was informed by an old gent walking his dog in 1994 that at the western end of the complex is an original tunnel running for a mile to a now filled quarry, although there was no evidence of it on my last descent.

Great Bardfield 167-010300 A. G. S.

14th century St. Mary's church has a number of grotesque lions and a centaur inside and out. Under the east-end chancel buttresses outside are two stones, one of them is a yard across and the other is 2 feet long, both are about `5 inches high. This could be a classic example of old sacred stones being incorporated into the 'new' holy edifice, although I cannot find any leys here.

Great Bromley 168-083263 A, D. TP.

The church of St. George is a magnificent structure dubbed the cathedral of the Tendring Hundred. The dedication is appropriate because the adversary beast of the saint are carved on the first pillar we meet inside. However, not only is St. George absent but the dragons are winning the battle! One dragon, of the wyvern species with a looped tail, has a woman's head in its mouth. A second conventional dragon - four legs and wings - has its jaws embedded in a man's face! It is accompanied on the other side of the head by a smaller lizard like animal doing the same while also digging its claws in. The man's head is very lifelike and his lack of expression does not match his predicament. In fact his tongue is poking out in the manner of a classic tongue poker - he clearly is not saying ouch!

The best explanation offered is that the human heads represent souls being tormented in hell, a reminder of what happens if not a regular church attender. But the facial styles, as mentioned, hardly depict such and are elsewhere often shown with grossly distorted features which would seem unnecessary if portraying ordinary folk. The church leaflet, incidentally, says that it portrays that the mason had a sense of humour - no better reasoning is forthcoming.

Great Burstead 167-681922 SC. TP.

St. Mary's church stands on a supposed Celtic druidic temple site and displays an enormous yew tree in the grounds to testify to its long usage. Yews, being evergreens with a long lifespan symbolise eternal life, resurrection and probably reincarnation.

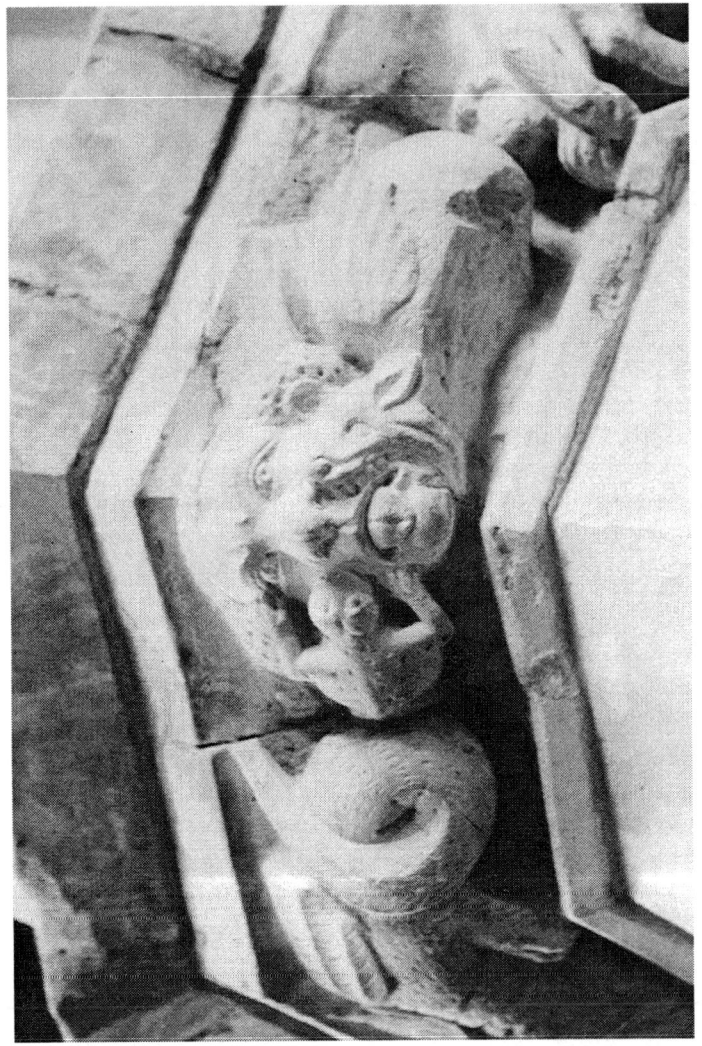

Great Bromley

Churchyards are often graced with one. The druids held yew foliage as special, and some still retain elements of folklore, such as; walking three times around one and pushing a pin into it will raise a ghost. On a practical side they were planted post-conquest so as to act as protection from the weather for the church porch.

Inside the building are two tongue pokers carved into wooden beams opposite as smiling Hagoday; a sun god face. Recently discovered murals of a south wall depict the fire goddess St. Catherine, to give the building a solar feel to it, perhaps reflecting its pagan past.

Great Canfield 167-595180 A. D. G. GM. EW. LL. P. S. SC.

St. Mary's church displays fine Norman door arch chevrons and further carvings that make it one of the most interesting in Essex. The tympanum over the south door has semi-circle and zig-zags carved to represent the sunrise. A modern reproduction is over the north door. On the right side porch pillar is a green man with foliage flowing from his mouth.

Opposite is another head of similar style but this man has a beard which two birds are pecking at. The church architecture reflects a Danish influence so this could portray the Norse god Odin/Woden with his ravens Hugin and Munin (thought and memory), who would be sent to wing the world every morning and question the living and the dead to keep Odin informed of all things amongst men.

Besides this is a neat row of five fylfots or swastikas. The swastika is a very old solar symbol used in many parts of the world, the name being sanscrit. The mosaic floor of the Roman villa at Lullingstone, Kent, has several of them. It is also a symbol of the Norse god Thor after which the day of Thursday was named. Being the fifth day of the week it may be why there are five fylfots, but the symbols were also adopted by early Christians.

Great Canfield

100

Great Canfield

On a window ledge slab inside we find some Celtic style horse head engravings. This slab was probably bought in ready carved when the church was built. This also applies to the burial slab that projects from the the capital of a chancel pillar of Anglo-Nordic Ringerike design showing a zoo-morphic style of the 11th century. This can be viewed by a mirror on a pole, provided.

On a circular bench end are two dragons. It is advisable to study these with a torch to appreciate their fine craftsman-ship. One is curled round on itself amidst flowers and foliage. The other is an unusual combination of a dragon with a face akin to a devil with horns, complete with clawed legs, wings and a scorpion-like body. It is amidst foliage like a green man and has stems issuing from its toothed mouth. Oddly, it also appears to have a forked tail, one side being curled and the other with the heraldic arrow head.

Elsewhere another dragon is biting its own tail and is of the type known as an Ouroburus of Nordic mythology. Often in serpent form too, it can be traced back to ancient Egypt, and is found world wide. Generally it means, 'all in one' or 'continuity'. Here it is known as Jormundgand the Midgard serpent that encircles the world of man. It is eventually killed by Odin who, however, eventually succumbs to the fatal poisonous breath of the creature. Here we may have the serpent shown as the usual symbol of elemental energy which, if destroyed will result in the same fate for the destroyer. In Chinese Feng Shui a 'stagnant' or destroyed ch'i force becomes 'sha' which is likened to a harmful breath. Dare I suggest that it is a message relevant today saying that if we destroy nature then we destroy ourselves?

An interesting feature of the church is the fresco of St. Mary and child on the east chancel wall. It was painted over, probably during the reformation, and depicts the child as a boy being breast fed on her knee. Of red and yellow ochre it was discovered late last century.

In the north wall is incorporated a stone, similar to that at Colne Engaine, of pagan origin.

The earthwork behind the church is a Norman mound about 50 feet high by 280 feet across with an outer area of 7 acres. It is thought to have already been a Saxon stronghold. Two leys that run through the church and the edge of the mound may suggest that it is older.

Great Chesterfield   154-505428 G.
All Saint's church has some notable gargoyles on the walls including a winged dog-like creature on a corner with huge claws, a snub nose and big eyebrows. Another is similar but is wingless and has large ears. A third beast is frog-like with huge eyes and bat-like wings or legs.

Great Dunmow   167-626227 A. G. GM.
The grand church of St. Mary has numerous animal heads and gargoyles on the outer walls. These include a bull head and an interesting 'pig' with short blunt horns. On the north side is a green man consisting of leaves. Further green men are visible high on the roof bosses inside.

Town Centre 167-628220 S.
Where three ways meet by the Star Inn, buried half in the wall of a shop opposite is a stone that is probably about 3 feet across. A ley line runs through it from the church.

Town Outskirts 167-626228 S.
This stone, measuring some 4 feet by 3 ft by 1 foot lay hidden for years in the undergrowth besides a three way junction near the church on the old A130. It has now been liberated so hopefully it will receive due respect. Legend has it that it jumps the flanking wall hence its name of the Jumping Stone. It is said that if a fair maiden should touch the stone then she will surely become heavy with child! Again we have this nationwide link of fertility and standing stone.

Great Chesterfield

Great Hallingbury 167-511196 S.
St. Mary's church has a stone laying on the grass verge outside the grounds standing 2 feet high.

Great Horkesley 168-981321 S.
Near the junction of Holly Lane is a house named Greenbank House with 7 or 8 large stones of limestone and sandstone decorating the garden. I do not know of their origin and they may be ploughed up from the surrounding fields. However, several show evidence of weathering as if once used then buried. Many are four or five feet long and one is 6 feet by 3 feet by 3 feet.

All Saints Church 168-971313 A.
The 14th century church has animal heads around the tower, one being an unusual open mouthed goat.

Great Leighs 167-728172 S.
In the car park of St. Anne's Castle pub, claimed to be the oldest used pub in the land, is a 2 foot stone called the Witches Stone, although the 'real' stone was much larger and is now gone, where to is not known. However, the remaining lump may be a chip off the old block. It originally came from the three ways meet nearby at Scrap Faggots Green, this colourful appelation being an old Essex name for a witch. In 1943 the road was widened to accommodate heavy traffic from the newly built American airbase at Boreham. The stone was moved against the wishes of villagers who claimed that it marked a witch's grave and thus to do so would invite bad luck.

According to Ian Dawson's article in *ASH* magazine, things did go badly. An Ann Hewghes was brought to trial at Chelmsford in 1621 for murder, and convicted also of petty treason, so was burned at the stake. Incidentally, witches were not burned in England for the crime of witchcraft, but hung or stoned. Ann was buried at a crossroads, a traditional witches burial place, and a stone was rolled over the grave to keep her down. Ash and bones were discovered on its removal. As a result of the violation odd

Great Dunmow

things are claimed to have happened. Haystacks fell and straw was scattered about neighbouring fields. Sheep got out of closed pens, and the church bells rang at midnight, the clock running slow. Builders found scaffolding poles spread about, and paint pots vanished along with tools. The pots were found under a bed in the attic of the cottage they were working on. Cows stopped giving milk, geese disappeared and wagons were found sideways in their sheds. Chickens stopped laying. An unknown stone turned up on the doorstep of the Dog and Gun pub.

Locals submitted that the witch's ghost was taking her revenge, and a psychic investigator was called in. This was none other than Harry Price, famous for his investigations at Borley Rectory in Essex, know as the most haunted house in England. He witnessed an event and suggested that the stone be put back on the grave. The villagers did so and all returned to normal, if not before a woman found her pet rabbits in with the chickens!

It would be interesting to fully verify this tale. Was the witch responsible as a poltergeist of causing the disturbances, or could a stone over a magnetic node point release an energy if moved?

The addenda to this tale is that the St. Annes Castle pub is said to be haunted by an old woman called Ann. A landlord who moved out in 1992 would testify that things had recently hotted up. The couple who took over featured on a video by Fred Curtis on the hauntings soon heard odd noises from one particular upstairs room, but were at the time undaunted.

Later that year a couple from Nottingham took it over to soon feature in a second video having already heard odd sounds. But apparently they were eventually driven out by the phenomena and a new landlord moved in, the brewers allowing the single man because of difficulties in getting somebody due to the situation. A woman took over the restaurant, and both were interested in actually investigating the hauntings.

Dave Hobbs and his wife attended a special meeting in 1995 thrown open to local psychics with the intention of allowing more

Great Sampford

people to link in to the building and, hopefully, learn of its past and identify the ghost.

The landlord experienced an inability to speak properly when showing visitors around. Since then new people have taken over the pub and are reluctant to exploit the build's risch history, so the nature of the hauntings remains a mystery.

Great Sampford   167-642353 A. G. P. TP.
St. Michael's church has numerous carvings including two fierce looking goats, two monkey heads and some tongue poking pigs, together with a hooded man and an owl. These are mainly found in a fascinating band of carvings around the capitol of a pillar. The vestry has a white tongue poker head that has been broken loose. The church was built by the Knights Hospitallers and has an odd painting that is fairly worn with six curving 'arms' on it.

Great Stambridge   178-894908 LL.
No gargoyles exist here at St. Mary and All Saints church on the shores of the River Roach. However, it is where a notable ley line commences, EX03, that runs to Canewdon church and on to Tiptree Rampart. Great Stambridge church is open during the day so it is possible for the reader to experience what appears to be an energy source beneath the building.

If you are a 'sensitive' or not, try standing about a yard in front of the altar. I am not very psychic but I once felt a sudden strong 'pull' as if a magnetic attraction was reacting to my body. It caused my trunk to twist and my knees to bend slightly. As with others, I have also felt as if I was shorter in height when standing on that spot. Dave Hobbs, my stone hunting companion, once felt an 'energy' coming into Canewdon church which was, unbeknown to him, along the direction of EX03 from Stambridge. I stood him on the altar spot, without informing him of what I had detected, and he felt that the atmosphere suddenly went 'silent' and then something like a force field or energy filled entity rushed in at him from the south, towards Canewdon, and

Great Waltham

literally knocked him sideways. He let out an oath that should not be heard in church and I had to jump out of his way because he is somewhat large in stature.

What is happening here is interesting. I am aware that many psychics are scatty, non-analytical 'new agers' prone to fantasy and whatever nonsense they get downwind of, so I steer well clear of them. Those I deal with are not hung up on which of their five assorted astral guides should be given the boot next, or see everything as roses and ice cream. So I feel safe in asserting that something exists at Stambridge. Some claim that medieval churches, when built on pagan sites, were positioned so that the altar was close to an energy node, as it seems to be here. There could be a strong blind spring, of water or ch'i energy here that reacts like attracting poles of a magnet to the human body in a spiral form; note that energies around standing stones spiral, too.

As for the 'entity' that Dave encountered, this could be what in psychic questing circles is known as the Genius loci, the guardian of the site, existing mostly in another dimension. This is speculated to be a basic life form created by an aware individual or formed by countless similar thoughts of the clergy and congregation, called thought forms. Or it could have been formed in pagan times. These are fairly well documented in Tibet where they are called Tulpas.

At Stambridge it would 'feed' off the node point and be formed out of what occultists term etheric material, one of the five bodies referred to by eastern doctrines, the base energy source of the human body, and that which is visible as a ghost.

Great Waltham   167-695134 A. D. G.
The large church of St. Mary and St. Lawrence is of Norman origin with some excellent carvings outside. The north wall has climbing animals and the south and east walls have gargoyles - remember here that the tower is always at the western end, churches mainly pointed to the sunrise of the day of the saint to

which it is dedicated. Amongst the best is a full bodied lion with odd twin toed hooves! There is a beautiful winged dog with huge ears and long, three toed clawed feet. It is notable that they are very similar to some at Kelvedon and Stansted churches. Perhaps the same mason was busy or the same theme was adopted. There is also a horned, griffin-like bird with large ears. Another feature is a large head of a three horned devil with a flat nose and winged cheeks. The old lych gate has two wyverns in the wooden arches plus two dragons issuing foliage from their mouths like green men.

Green Street   167-573192 S.

Near Puttocks End and where three roads meet at Pecker's Farm is are two stones on the grass verge. One is of limestone and is 2 feet high and may have ancient significance because a ley line runs through it and another begins here, running to Great Canfield. The other stone, of a different colour, was dumped here in 1993 probably a plough find.

Hadleigh   178-810860 EW.

Occupying several acres overlooking the Thames, Hadleigh Castle was built at about 1231 by Hubert de Burgh, High Justiciar of England and Baron of Rayleigh. After surviving its only siege of the Peasant's revolt in 1381 it lost its military value and fell into ruins. Low walls and a battered tower shell are all that remain.

The site is not supposed to belong to any earlier age but an interesting ghost story and a ley line cutting its western rim promote its inclusion to this book. Philip Benton, a local 19th century historian tells of a milkmaid named Sally who worked at Castle Farm many years before. At dawn one day she met the ghost of a white lady on the castle grounds. The white lady commanded her to return there at midnight so that she could disclose 'mysteries connected there with'. But Sally did not find the courage to meet the ghost so did not turn up that night. In the morning the milk maid met the white lady who bitterly

unbraided he for not coming and so cuffed Sally round the ear in her anger. So hard was the blow that it almost dislocated her neck, so hence forth she was known as Wry Neck Sal!
The interesting aspect of this story is that it speaks of mysteries connected with the castle. This may suggest that the site may have some 'geomantic' validity to qualify its listing.

Thought to be buried in unconsecrated ground in Hadleigh churchyard - at 810870 - is James 'cunning' Murrell, a local wise man/wizard character who lived in the last century. He acted as the vet for the area farms, and was also an astrologer and herbalist so often seen in the fields around the castle collecting ingredients for his potions. He took an interest in astronomy and anatomy as his many hand written books testify. He is supposed to have predicted his own death down to the minute. Southend museum has one of his note books and Southchurch Hall, a medieval site that is now a colourful, moated museum and park, has his trunk in which he stowed magical implements.

Hadstock 151-559448 S.

This village has a pretty triangular green that is edged with white painted stones. About 13 are of a size too big to pick up, the largest is over two feet long. Two more rounded boulders sit by a farm entrance a little higher up the Suffolk bound road, and another, but a foot or so across, marks a tiny junction. A further flat stone of some 18 inches sits by a farm gate on the east bound Linton road a stones throw away. A ley runs through the green from Barley, Herts.

Halstead 154-515307 G. TP.

St. Andrew's church has some animal style gargoyles around its tower. The 19th century St. James at the other end of town is unusual in that it has continued the gargoyles tradition with a high frieze of heads including a tongue poker.

Harlow 167-477112 T.
It is believed that Roman dignatories were buried at a barrow here but it is not listed on the O/S map of Roman Britain.

Hatfield Broad Oak 167-547166 S.
The main street of this rural village plays host to three stones lying on the pavements. None are more that 15 inches across. The two on the south side are puddingstones and the other is of a quartz variety on the opposite side, half buried and next to a brick wall. A ley includes this cluster en route to Little Easton church.

St. Mary's Church 167-547166 D.
Inside this church, the successor of a Saxon building, can be found a carving of St George and the dragon.

Hawkwell 178-841915 S.
On private land, this 3 foot high stone was restood by its owner in 1980 and dubbed the 'Venus Stone' because he felt it resembled a statue of the goddess of that name. It was last known to be standing at around 1850 and is surely a mark stone. It is on a 7 point ley line and comes complete with a reputation of being a 'growing' stone, an appelation connected with stones across the land.

Many artifacts have been unearthed on this site - that is edged on one side by a now filled and levelled ditch and bank - including a Mesolithic mase head indicating that the area could have been in continual use for 7000 years. An on site well adds evidence to this hypothesis.

Henham 167-544287 A. D. G. GM. S. TP.
This village has a pitted limestone megalith outside a picturesque farm house to the north of the church measuring over 4 ft x 2 ft 6" x 18". To the south of the church are two more

in front of some farm yard stables. One is about 2 foot square and the other a yard long, both are lying flat. These stones fall onto a ley line that includes stones at Lindsell and Bardfield Saling churches. Besides a cottage by the church gate is a much smaller stone.

St. Mary's church has two round grotesque heads on the porch, with a larger devil like head similar to one at Great Dunmow. Inside, on a frieze above the pillars is a pig's head. The wooden rood screen is worth close scrutiny so as to find a tongue poking face with curly hair, a green man and several dragons. These carving are delightfully reflected on the kneeling cushions, many sewn by the local Girl Guides.

Several dragon legends are linked with Henham, one as late as 1668 when a horseman, of worthy reputation, encountered it near Birch Wood. It angrily hissed and lunged at him. The farmer who owned the land called for volunteers to despatch the beast, but they were thin on the ground! Two others then saw it basking in the sun and got a good look at it, describing it as 9 feet long with small wings, sharp eyes and excellent rows of teeth. A man armed himself with a gun, but the creature had gone, then on reappearing it seemed harmless. Some say that the story was a hoax in order to explain the church dragons - such things are sometimes an embarrass-ment to the Church.

High Easter   167-624149 S.
At the road junction by a triangular green lies a stone on the grass verge with a notable upward curve at one end. It is 3 ft 6" long and on a ley line running to Pleshey earthwork.

St. Mary's Church   167-620148 D. G. S.
The building is of Saxon origin and has some fine examples of animal type gargoyles on its north side. One is a dog-like beast with large nostrils, a wide mouth and prominent eye ridges. In the church grounds lies a diamond shaped stone about 2 ft 6" long. Several leys run to it.

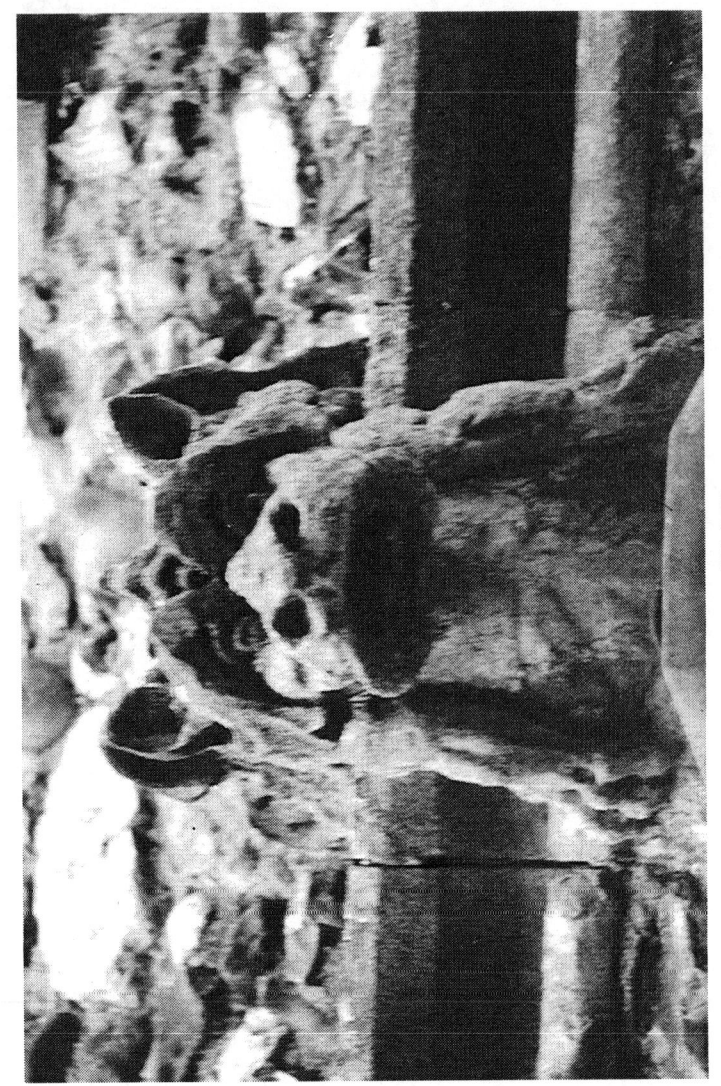

High Easter

High Laver 167-525079 S.
Flanking the entrance drive to Bushes Farm and on a ley line are three stones. One is a puddingstone conglomerate over four feet long and the others are smaller and of sandstone.

Hobbs Cross 167-494102 S.
This tiny village near Harlow has a small stone 18 inches high on the grass verge outside Hobbs Hurst House. A hobb is an old name for the devil or an imp or demon. The term cross usually depicts a preaching cross so it is possible that the stone is the remains of one. A ley runs through it coming up from the stone at Copthall Green. A friend and I found the stone by literally concluding that the village name indicated that there should have once been something pagan there - and there was. The fact that my friend's name is Dave Hobbs helped to make the day.

Hockley 178-840933 T.
North of the town on a hill top is Plumberow Mount tumulus, about 16 feet high and 55 feet across, on which once stood a Victorian Summerhouse. Excavations in 1914 revealed some Roman and Saxon pottery, but being as it is also considered to be Danish or British we can see that dating it is but guess work. It has no burial finds and so may be of the Bronze Age because an 8 point ley, KT51, from Kent, passes through it, and another ends here coming over the river from Bushey Hill and Danbury.

Hornchurch 177-544870 A.
The village, now a London suburb town, derived its name, some say, from St. Andrew's church. Outside, on the apex of the chancel is a large stone bull's head with long horns.

The village is first mentioned in 1222 by way of a reference to a horned church or monastery at Havering. But the origin of the name and the bull is a mystery. The head may have come from the seal of the Abbey of Montjoux to whom, Henry 11 gave a grant of land. A church stood on the site in 1163, and it may have been then when, according to one story, the king's dogs killed a hart, and the horns were put into the church.

Many tales exist as to the origin of the horns, be they from a bull or a deer. In 1610 the horns were said to be made of lead but much later in 1824 they were found to be of copper. We are talking bull's horns here yet in 1604 the village was known as Herne Church, so the original horns seem to have been antlers because Herne is a Celtic horned god of the forest with stag's antlers. Some say that the building was put up by tanners who placed bull's horns upon the church as their sign.

A further story tells of a local lady of the manor who sold her body to raise building funds at the rate of one session per stone! A variation has her paying for the church after converting her faith as a repentance for her sinful past. The place thus became known as Horechurch until a passing king changed it to Hornchurch.

Another colourful tale relates how a man returning home across an adjoining field was attacked by a wild boar. A huge bull appeared and chased the boar off, but then turned on him. He was able to kill the bull but felt sad afterwards because it had saved his life. So in honour of the beast he had the horns hung on the church. Another version says that it was the prior who was attacked by a bull on his way to church and that a herd of cows saved him by surrounding the bull.

Horndon-on the-Hill 177-669833 G.

The church of SS Peter and Paul was built on an earlier pagan site. The oldest section of the building is the tower, the door arch of which displays two heads within a design like four petals of flowers. These could be a remnant of the Celtic head cult because they resemble no known person or deity. At the opposite end of the church is a head carving known as the ugly woman of Horndon, although her identity is not known.

Ingatestone 167-651997 LL. S.
This town straddling the old A12 has a scattering of 6 stones close to the church of SS Edmund and Mary. When the church nave was renovated a sarsen stone was dug up measuring 2 feet across. Don't be misled by the church guide when it tells us that its a puddingstone and on the north side of the building rather than the south side.

This stone may have some lingering energy despite being moved. On crouching besides it to check it with a compass I placed a hand lightly on it. I felt a kind of electric shock that spun me round so that I nearly landed on my backside. This effect with stones has been felt by other researchers. It a sensation rather like placing the same poles of two magnets together, and similar to that effect felt at Great Stambridge church if simply standing in front of the altar.

At Ingatestone a 2 foot stone lies further north under a courtyard arch. In the main street two stones flank the Fryerning road at the junction. They actually protrude through the pavement to a height of a couple of feet. This graphically indicates the reverence given to these monoliths. They have got a preservation order on them so the council cannot move the incongruous blocks that rear in defiance like guardians of the three ways.

In the market square outside Lipton's supermarket are two more emissaries of the past. They are very small and can be easily missed despite being painted white. A 7 point ley line, EX06, runs through the church and the junction stones from Gray's dene holes and the Bulpham stone then on to the stone at Blackwall Bridge.

Kelvedon 168-856186 G.
The parish church of St. Mary is a must for all gargoyle fans with around 25 examples in good condition. They ring the tower and line friezes on the main building, two of these being very low, affording close inspection. A tower carving is a human head with long animal ears and leaves sprouting from its cheeks. Two

Ingatestone

artistic styles alternate elsewhere. One is a rotund face with large eyes similar to those at Prittlewell. The other are delightful and beautifully sculptured dog-like gargoyles. Each one is slightly different but all depict anatomically well proportioned animals crouching with their forepaws before them. On the north east corner is a head with fins growing from its cheeks.

Laindon 178-681985 D.

The 13th century church of St. Nicholas crests a hill thought to be a pagan site. Although the claim by a local historian that a stone circle once stood here, it is doubtful; circles just don't crop up on hilltops. However, a single stone may have graced the height because in accord to Feng Shui sitings such a hill would be a yang point amidst a flat 'yin surround' as at near by Pitsea. As with many Chinese hill tops this crest is artificially shaped.

Inside the church porch we find two dragons, one of which is breathing fire and resembles a crocodile with a cross piercing its back. The other wood carving is very different with what looks like crowns along its back and a knot in its tail.

Lambourne 167-479960 LL. S.

On the edge of a green near the rebuilt church is a stone measuring 2 ft x 2 ft. In the churchyard of the originally Norman church is a lone Scots Pine, so frequently found to mark leys by Watkins. Ley HF135 passes through here from Broxbourne church in Herts to the well at North Ockendon via the Cophall Green stone.

Latton 167-465107 D. G. TP.

St. Mary's church was pre-Norman and has tongue pokers around the tower doorway and the north side windows. We can also find a blocked north door. This practise seems to be the result of a change of policy inaugurated but a few hundred years ago. The north door was considered the 'pagan' door through

Kelveden

which those of that persuasion would enter the church. Perhaps when the church became more Christian orientated it became superfluous? Church lore says that it is the north door through which evil was allowed to exit during child baptisms.

Somewhere along the line they changed their minds, but why these portals are not simply locked other than bricked up, as a lot are, is one of the many unknowns with the Church today.

The weather vane at Latton is not the usual cockerel but a dragon.

Lawford   168-081319 T.
Rising to only a few feet on the edge of a field lays a rabbit-warrened tumulus some 50 feet across. I known nothing of its age.

Lindsell   167-643271 A. S.
Originally Norman this tiny church is hidden behind farm buildings. On either side of the western window are carvings of wild boar heads. By the corner of a barn is a stone some 18 inches high that may have ancient significance.

Little Baddow   167-764081 D. G.
St. Mary's church has remains of Roman and Saxon work in the walls. The tower has gargoyle heads and a stained glass window has St. Michael and the dragon.

Little Bardfield   167-656308 LL. S.
At the entrance to the drive of this chiefly Saxon church is a small stone. A hundred yards along the main road besides a brick wall, in the Great Bardfield direction, is another about 2 ft 6" long and knee high. It appears to be some sort of limestone conglomerate. Ley line EX93 from Clavering in the west runs to both the stones after hitting a tumulus east of Thaxted.

Little Braxted 168-836148 D. P.
Although the 12th century church of St. Nicholas has no carvings it is worth a visit to view its 19th century paintings that give a good idea of what all churches were once decorated like. The murals that cover most of the interior were by the hand of the Revd. Geldart done in 1881 to 84. The artist depicted the Creed in the form of a vine linking the saints. Centrally Christ is holding a long cross with which he is killing a dragon like serpent.

Little Burstead 178-668917 S.
Standing in a quiet country lane St. Mary's church dates from the 13th century. Lying by the porch are two stones that came from the church of Great Burstead and are the remains of a Saxon preaching cross. From St.Mary's we can see clearly across country to Great Burstead church along ley line EX59s which then goes on to Downham church and the Running Well.

Littlebury 154-518396 S.
Close to the double bend in the village are scattered 7 stones. Three are in a private garden, the largest being 3 ft x 3 ft x 1 ft and is of a triangular shape. The remainder are littered about by street buildings on pavements. Some are fairly small with one by a gate that is thigh high.

Ringhill Camp 154-517381 EW. LL.
The earthwork here covers an area of 18 acres with a circumference of 3300 feet. It is emersed in trees and surrounded by a 50 foot wide ditch and a rampart. It appears to have been occupied by the Romans whose coins have been found there, but it is undoubtedly older than that. Ley line EX176 that runs through it from Little Chesterfield church to Newport church via the Leper stone cuts along the western edge as leys tend to. The land is private but the southern rim is visible from the Strethall road.

Little Dunmow 167-656212 A. D. GM.
St. Mary's was once the priory church of the 12th century, destroyed in the dissolution. On the outer walls are a cat and a dog and a pig. Inside is a wyvern and various farm animals on panels. There is also a hag-like woman holding what could be a book while she strokes a cat. A witch and her familiar, maybe? A green man can also be found.

Little Hallingbury 167-492177 EW. LL.
By far the largest and most impressive site in Essex, Wallbury Camp lies wedged between the overgrown River Stort and a narrow road to Spellbrook just over the Herts border. It extends 1900 feet by 1550 feet covering 35 acres, making it bigger than Ambresbury and Loughton camps put together, and also of a greater area than most of the more renown camps in Hampshire and Wiltshire. Typically, Wallbury Dells, as it is known locally, is seldom mentioned in literature despite its size and, no doubt, one-time importance.

It is mainly obscured by bushes and trees including some mighty oaks, and is eroded in parts and difficult to gain access to as well as being on private land. It is divided into several fields inside with farm buildings and stables in the northern corner. its very size also acts to reduce its visual magnificence.

Its eastern, Essex facing side gives us the best picture of what it must have been like in its hayday. Two causeways drive across, one serving a metalled road, although it is not known if these are original or how many there once were. Twin ramparts are visible, rising five or six feet above ground level and either side of a 20 foot ditch that is nearly twice that width.

Its age is not known but considered to be Iron age, built by the local Trinovante tribe as an outpost as protection against the rival Catuvunlaunis from across the Stort. Ancient Britons could have retreated here from the Romans and it is one of the sites where Queen Boudicca is thought to have driven her chariot across its causeways. However, as with many an earthwork, its position is not ideal for defensive purposes. The land to the east is of a higher elevation. The camp itself is almost a mile in circumference so would probably require a force the size of four Roman legions to defend it, large enough, one would think, to negate the need to retreat. Again, if the British tribes had that sort of man power available to man just one fort then it would be doubtful if the Romans could have gained a foothold in the first place.

Three leys that I have found skirt the south and south-east ramparts.

Little Laver   167-545097 SC.
St. Mary's church was built in the 13th century and has some unusual carvings on its font in the same fashion as found at Abbess Roding and Fryerning. The consist of crescent moons, spiral suns and six pointed 'stars'.

Little Sampford   167-653337 S. SC.
In the grounds of St. Mary's church is a mark stone that has been converted into a tombstone. Engraved in a door pillar at the tower base is a six pointed device like a six pointed star within a ring. It may be a solar symbol related to those found on the fonts of Abbess Roding and Little Laver but it is also identical to a pagan hex (spell) symbol once used on all manner of buildings. This sign confers protection to the structure. Although the word is German for witch it is also Greek for six. This number has significant overtones in cosmic mathematics and ancient religious values. It is the number of points in a snow flake, the number of the Egyptian creator; Atum Ra, and it is found in the Star of David and in a bee's honeycomb.

Little Waltham   167-713128 LL. SC.
The church of St. Martin is a Victorian rebuild so of little interest carving wise. However, inside the bell tower is an engraving of a maze. There is also a graffiti fylfot inside. The building is

supposed to be on the site of a pagan temple and in support of this claim the church has four ley lines running through it. Intersight visibility would have been possible. The nearest known site is Great Waltham church just over a mile away. To the south a ley courses to the Cursus and may have needed another high ground site between them.

Loughton 167-419975 EW.
Discovered in Epping Forest in 1872 Loughton Camp is a 12 acre earth site with a well inside. Two leys start/finish here. It is probably pre-Iron age and related to Ambresbury Banks to the north.

Magdelen Laver 167-513083 S.
St. Mary Magdelen church is built on two small puddingstones that are visible under the north side wall. Laying flat at the east end of the church is a slab of limestone 8 inches thick and 4.5 ft in height. According to Dr Rudge of the Essex Field Club it came from a field a few hundred yards to the west. Further over, on the road outside Hall Farm at ref 510083 is another small stone. It may have been dug from a field but is on a ley line to the church.

Maggots End 167-486277 LL. S.
A puddingstone block 3ft x 3 ft x 2ft sits at a road junction to Pinchpools House. It is on a ley line - EX158 - that includes two more stones, including the mark stone at Manuden, the church of which can be seen from the Maggots End stone.

Maldon 168-839073 T.
In a field south of the 12th century Beeleigh Abbey, now a private house, is a saucer barrow of considerable diameter if very low. It is thought to be either Saxon or Danish but it is uncertain. Two leys run through it, one of them from the Green Street stone that continues on to Asheldham Camp.

Magdalene Lever

Manuden 167-491267 S.
Besides the road by the churchyard wall is a limestone block 3 feet long by nearly 2 feet across. It stands on the edge of an oval, pre-Christian site on which was built St. Mary's church. Over the road by the Yew Tree Inn stands another stone, this one of the pudding variety rising to a height of 4 feet. These stones are on ley EX158 that runs about a mile north to the puddingstone at Maggots End.

Margaretting 167-665005 GM.
Inside St. Margaret's church are two green men in the nave corners. They have teeth and sprout two oak leaves each.

Mashbury 167-652119 CA. S.
The old Norman church is now privately owned. It stands close to Mashbury Hall and is in a pretty setting close to a duck pond. its porch door has some fine examples of Norman zig-zag work, the meaning of which is not known. Close by stands a large puddingstone listed by Dr. Rudge as being on his "puddingstone trail" - a run of stones across several counties. It stands 4 feet high by 2 feet across. A possible ley runs through it taking in 4 sites in three miles from Good Easter church to Chignall Smealey stones. The line includes a possible site at Wares Farm at ref:638119. Around 13 stones lie here next to a moated house, mostly retrieved from the fields, but several larger ones have been there for a long time and may be mark stones.

Matching 167-525120 GM. MP. TP.
St. Mary's church is of Saxon origins with the present building of 13th century vintage. Inside is a green man with a single leaf poking from each side of his mouth. Several mouth pullers are to be found. One of these is a two headed man with his hands facing opposite directions. This figure is using two hands to pull one mouth while the other has one hand to the mouth and the second gripping his foot which is across his chest. This may be something to do with the twin headed Roman god Janus who is

the god of doorways and public gates - the figure is by the door. Two faces allowed him to see inside and out of the house at the same time. He is also a solar god ruling over the day, and the month of January is named after him.

The action with the foot, however may indicate that he represents the Summer Oak King who is symbolic of the year after the winter solstice. He would have been ritually slain in rural festivals by the winter Holly King. Later the king is not sacrificed but lamed. Is this why the figure is holding his foot? This guide book describes them as two men with toothache!

Messing   168-897183 T.
A short way off the road into some woods is a tumulus some 5 feet high by about 50 feet across. All I know of it is that in spring it is covered in bluebells.

Mile End   168-990276 EW.
This earth rampart in High Woods may well be Roman although it does not appear on the ordnance map of Roman Britain.

Mistley   168-114318 G.
Although St. Mary's church is a 19th century replacement in 14th century style for the ruined church at Mistley Heath, it has tower gargoyles probably rescued from the old building. They are four legged beasts with devil-like heads. Each one has variations in the composition of its ears and horns.

Moreton   167-537070 S.
At the road junction in this rustic village are three stones. One is painted white, and the largest is about knee high. These stones demonstrate the veneration they still command, two of them act as obstacles on the narrow pub rimming pavement. They don't really look pretty or impressive yet they survive still as ambassadors of the past.

Moulsham 167-720055 S.

A hamlet at one time more important than its tiny neighbour of Chelmsford, and now swallowed in the sprawl of the latter, perhaps it is not too surprising that we should find a stone here. It sits in the car park of a pub on the old A130 near a three way meet, measuring 33" x 28" at its widest points. I have not yet found any leys running to it.

Mount Bures 168-904325 EW. S.

This village derives its name from the artificial mound backing on to the parish church. Of unknown origin it once supported a Norman keep, and covers 1.5 acres with a height of 45 feet although it was once about 80 feet. A 10 foot ditch rims it and it is covered with a mantle of trees. It presents an impressive sight and not one we would expect to find in a county like Essex.

Laying by the churchyard wall is a puddingstone, but it has no geomantic value having been unearthed by the plough about 30 years ago. However, I learned this while in conversation with a farm hand. What he told Dave Hobbs and I underlined the influence that stones still hold over us. He said that he asked the land owner if he could keep the attractive, newly dug stone for a garden ornament, not knowing, incidentally, that it was natural stone. He told us that the farmer quite firmly refused his request, insisting that it should be deposited by the churchyard wall. And so it was. The story teller said that his wife actually put it there. This later caused Dave and I to smile on reflection because the impression was given that the woman had literally manhandled the stone. As it must weigh something like 70lbs we wondered if she was an ex Russian shot putter!

Intrigued as to why the farmer should insist on the particular location for the stone, I put the question to the farmhand. He immediately became almost agitated, acting very uncomfortably defensive to the query as if he'd been 'caught out' or found it embarrassing. Almost in a fluster he replied that the farmer was a strict man, if fair in his ways, before completing his answer by extolling the man@s other virtues.

Mount Bures

Of course my question was unanswered, indeed it seemed almost deliberately avoided. This was odd. He reacted as do the Church clergy sometimes when the subject of pagan carvings if encrouched, they become prickly and evasive. Our man ducked the issue of the farmer's reasons yet we had told him what we were interested in, and he was not adverse to discussing stones or ley lines and the like.

So what compels a farmer - as I have also found elsewhere - having just dented a plough blade and spent valuable time moving the offending obstacle, too, instead of dumping it contemptuously out of sight, treat it with what appears to be reverence. So often these boulders are stood in a prominent position for all to see. Not to mention the case at Mount Bures where the stone is considered to 'belong' to the church grounds. A holy stone to a holy place?

To 'ice the cake' as it were, we had asked if any other stones existed in the vicinity. Our answer was, again, not too concise, it appeared that another puddingstone was found and hidden by the farmer in his barn so that nobody would bother him asking to look at it. Apart from that we were assured that there were none around.

On leaving, we drove south, only to find that a few hundred yards away was a sandstone block about waist high standing as bold as brass on the grass verge by the entrance to a farm! Stones cast mysteries indeed. This stone shows a lot of wear so maybe it is in its original position. It is, incidentally, mentioned in Tom Graves, *Needles of Stone*. However, the ley mentioned is not too valid and the stone is erroneously said to be in Suffolk.

Mountnessing 167-648967 GM. LL.

St. Gile's church is one of those built some distance from the village making us wonder why the impracticality. Inside is a green man carving described in one Essex village guide book as a woman with a band across her mouth! Ley line EX06 passes through the church from Pleshey, running through a small wood to the south in which towers a classic 'Watkins' ley point, a solitary Scots Pine.

Mucking 177-685811 GM.

The 13th century church of St.John the Baptist is one of a growing number now redundant and in private hands. Let us hope that at least the more interesting ones survive intact. Not only are they an example of the oldest remaining structures - if one discounts chambered barrows - in the land, but if demolished and built over we lose what is often a sacred site as old as anywhere in the world. Mucking in particular appears to have a churchyard that is raised above the surrounding fields.

Inside the church carvings on the capital of a pillar show a Moon goddess and a green man with foliage adjoining the pair. On the other side of the pillar is a horned female face within a horseshoe encompassed by a circle and topped by a crescent moon.

The odd name of the village simply stems from Saxon origins - as do 90% of Essex names - meaning the settlement of the people of Mucca.

Mundon 168-880032 GV. S.

The tiny hidden church of St. Mary is now disused and being restored. Its chief feature is its unusual hexagonal timber belfry tower. It is worth trying to psychically 'tune in' to this old building. Twice I was inside when the door appeared to close behind me because the light faded, but the door had not moved and no clouds obscured the sun. Others have felt an odd 'atmosphere'.

A ley may end here indicating an energy point. A small stone lies half hidden in the grounds by the south wall but of an unknown origin.

Behind the church to the east is what is believed by researcher John Ruse to be a long abandoned grove of oaks. Over 20 huge dead trunks form a stark wide ring in a field close to Mundon Hall. No doubt hundreds of years old, the ring could have been a survivor of pre-Roman times because of the practise of continual replanting when trees died.

Navestock 167-550983 EW. LL.
Obscure within the confines of what was once called Fortification Wood is an earthwork of unknown age. The area occupies 4 acres and is surrounded in parts by a 6 foot ditch. At the northern end is a pond. Two leys run through it, one including the earthwork at Pilgrims Hatch and the other at Ambresbury Banks in Epping Forest.

Newport 154-520537 S.
Rising boldly by the old A11 near Newport is the Leper Stone. Tradition claims that it got its name from when alms were left on it for lepers in the Middle Ages. However, the word may be a corruption of leaping denoting supposed movement of the stone as with the jumping or leaping stone at Great Dunmow. It is, allowing for the recumbent at Ovington, the largest standing stone in Essex being 4 ft 6" wide by 4 foot tall. Being a foot thick it must weigh nearly two tons. It sits on ley line EX176 that runs for only 4.5 miles from Newport church to Little Chesterfield church taking in Ring Hill earthwork.

Northey Island 168-881096 T.
Situated on a lonely island in the mouth of the River Blackwater is a tumulus of unknown age. A testimony to its antiquity may lie in the fact that ley line EX102.5 runs here from Lucus farm to Beeleigh Abbey and onto Beacon Hill. A second ley passes through Beeleigh Abbey and ends on the island.

North Ockendon 177-586849 LL. W.
At the rear of St. Mary Magdelen church is the holy well of St. Cedd the first Bishop of Essex. The old name of the village was

Newport Leper Stone

North Ockendon Septfontaines which refers to seven springs. The location of the other six is uncertain; locals cite various locations, one being called Hobbs Hole, a pond about a kilometre away. The survivor by the church has a wooden decorated canopy over it featuring Mary Magdelen and a male figure. Mike Batley told me that some years ago he met an elderly woman who looked after it. She told him that the male figure once had horns that were erased because the Church authorities frowned upon them! It is possible to detect them today even if they look like traces of ears. Maybe they originally represented a god and goddess?

Perhaps as evidence that the well is special, there are 4 ley lines which cross here, three terminating.

Orsett 177-651807 CC
Now barely visible in a ploughed field is one of only two such earthworks in Essex, the other being at Springfield. The Orsett site is marked on the O/S map as a Neolithic Camp.

Ovington 154-763426 S.
Lying behind a hedge outside the churchyard by a residential entrance road is a huge lump of limestone measuring just under 6 feet by 4 ft 2" and probably weighing 4 tons. This is the largest stone in Essex if of genuine ancient usage and not simply a plough find.

Pilgrims Hatch 177-578947 EW.
Now not too easily definable as an earthwork it covers about 7 acres with a road running through it. its age has not been defined.

Pitsea 178-738878 HH.
This hill top church is inevitably dedicated to St. Michael being as it is an extremely prominent rise of over 120 feet above the

surrounding marsh flat. St. Michael's Mount would appear to be a well balanced site in terms of Feng Shui. The church is unfortunately now a ruin. Excavations on the hill have revealed what is considered to be a holy spring. A probable standing stone has been found along with Iron Age pottery.

Pleshey 167-663143 EW.
The ramparts in this village cover an area only just second in size to Wallbury Camp. Visitors will be attracted to the 50 foot high motte and its two acre bailey with a moat on the south side. The foundations of the motte, now accessible via a remarkable 15th century brick bridge, are Saxon, and were heightened by the Normans for a fortification. After this the site was taken over by the nobility, and a stone keep was constructed. By the 16th century this was a ruin and only the foundations remain. To the north of the motte is thought to be a lower bailey on which now stands many of the village houses.

Beyond this earth complex curves the outer low rampart 1500 feet in diameter. Pleshey is rich in medieval history, mostly skulduggery and conflict, yet many question marks remain as to the precise nature of events of this period. The town, according to historian, Leyland, was once called Tumblestoun, or town of the tumulus suggesting that the mottle was similar to the mounds at Rayleigh and Stebbing. Pleshey appears to be a typical multiple overlay construction of consecutive ages with probably every possibility of it dating back to earliest times.

Three ley lines help to suggest great age, skirting the rims as per 'tradition'.

Holy Trinity Church 167-662143 G.
The village church is outside the earthwork and has a ring of gargoyles at the top of the tower. These are fine examples of ugly cat-like creatures leaning out from the corners.

Plesheybury 167-648144 S.
Until 1995, at a point where three ways meet on the road west of Pleshey, was a recumbent stone on the grass verge. It measures about 2 foot 6 inches long and is partly buried. It is probably a mark stone in the true later sense because it stands on a corner of a parish boundary. The question is, what came first, the boundary or the stone? Ley line EX102 may suggest the latter because it ends here having taken in another three stones and Wallbury Camp, making it one of the few Essex leys that contain edifices solely of the Neolithic period.

Since Ian Dawson first acquainted me with this stone, another two have joined it. But I suspect farmers rather than stone age shamans are responsible. The three are all now on the central triangle of grass.

Prittlewell 178-877873 CA, LL. W.
The Cluniac priory served the village which is in the mother parish of Southend, the town being at the south end of Prittlewell. The priory was founded in 1100 and the surviving buildings are now a museum. Above the north door of the refractory is a particularly well preserved example of Norman zig-zag carvings and foliage work. Of the place name we have a little confusion. Some references say that it means babbling brook, and Prittlebrook meanders pleasantly through the park in which the priory stands. Yet this source fails to mention the well. A well does exist but under the road by the western entrance to the park, the old iron pump remaining up to the 1960s. But the well could be the natural spring that now feeds the duck paddled ponds dug as fisheries by the monks.

It is over this spring that three leys pass. One of them. EX67, is only six miles long with five points. Commencing at Leigh church it runs through the park to Sutton Camp, the ruins of Shopland church at ref 899883 and then to Barling church.

St. Mary's Church 178-877867 D. G. MP. TP.
The parish's medieval church is a grand example of the

perpendicular style with its multi sectioned tower. Built of Kentish ragstone in also has traces of Saxon work in one wall. It has a few surviving gargoyles, two of these being tongue pokers, one has what appears to be laurel leaves on its head like a Roman Emperor. High on the tower are a few mouth pullers. The stained glass windows in the porch unusually depict King Arthur and Sir Galahad. Both St. Michael and St. George are also here, the latter shown 'defeating' moslems who cower before the hooves of his horse. But he is shown holding the lance the wrong way round, as if offering it to them in a gesture of peace. St. Michael's dragon is bound in golden chains.

Purleigh 168-840015 EW.
Near the church is an entrenched mound about 150 feet across and 6 feet high surrounded by a 12 foot wide ditch and outer ramparts of low height. The whole site is overgrown, not marked on any map and furbishes a commanding view of the countryside. I know nothing of its age but it is on a ley that includes the church. More significantly relevant is the fact that the outer rampart is thus, not inside the ditch, indicating that it was not an Iron Age defensive site and thus older.

Quendon 167-516315 T.
Within the private grounds of Quendon Park is a mound of unknown age.

Rayleigh 178-807909 EW. LL.
Marked on the maps as a castle, although no stone building remains here. Rayleigh Mount is a National Trust site of some 2 acres comprising a Norman motte and bailey up to 50 feet in height. A 30 ft wide moat, with ducks, still rings about half of it.

The Normans are generally said to have been the sole builders of this earthwork, but having known it for many years I was always dubious of this claim. If it was Norman, and thus defensive, then it is odd why it is reached by a downhill path on the town side.

Furthermore, the highest point of the natural knoll on which much of Rayleigh stands is occupied by the church of 1380.

The site guide plaque makes no suggestion of it being pre-Norman. Most sources say that the church and Hadleigh castle were constructed from stone salvaged from the ruins of the mount, yet the castle was a wooden keep. Stone is said to have been used for paving but it would hardly be enough to supply these later demands.

Finding an old 1930s guide to Southend by Donald Glennie I found that my suspicions appear to be correct. During the reign of Edward the Confessor, prior to the conquest, the site is referred to as the 'ruined castle', and that it was probably a pre-Roman earthwork reshaped by the Saxons. During this phase, Glennie says that it had earth walls 100 feet high with a 50 foot deep moat. Such information is typical of much of the contradiction found within this subject.

To further confuse the issue, in Arthur Mee's *Essex*, we find an odd reference to an earthwork of a prehistoric race on the ridge of a hill. Having already mentioned the mount he appears to allude to a further site. I can only assume that either Mee is mistaken or that the earthwork encompassed the whole hill crest to include the church and the mound. If so it might explain the relatively low position of the castle against that of the church even though the latter was preceded by another building.

If the two sites were one then it would also fit in with the tracks of six leys that visit here. Only Rochford, according to my findings, has as many, more than any other site in Essex. A line starts here and runs up to Stow Maries church. another comes in from Great Burstead church and continues to Rochford itself. Others come from Ramsden Bellhouse church, Wickford church and Fobbing church. The sixth is EX79 from North Benfleet and on to the Venus Stone.

The church itself, that takes on two of these leys, has no gargoyles despite its size. It did have a good example of a

141

bricked up north door, now reused after many years to allow access to a church hall on the site.

Ridgewell 154-737409 S.
On the typically English village green is a mark stone possibly indicating a three way meet. It stands thigh high close to the old well pump. A three foot stone lies by a garden wall close by. Half a mile to the north where three ways meet at Bowles Farm are two sandstones lost in the grass, both a couple of feet long. The grid reference is 738414.

Rochford 178-873903 CA. G. LL. TP.
St. Andrew's church can - as far as I have found - claim more ley lines than any site in Essex allowing for the double site at Rayleigh, 6 in all. EX170n is a good example. From Prittlewell Priory it goes through Rochford to the site of a Preaching cross, then Ashingdon church and on to Beeleigh Abbey. EX109s from Toot Hill to Great Wakering church takes it in, too. Most of the 8 intermediate ley points are still intervisible today.

The church itself has three surviving grotesque heads, one of these being a tongue poker, another is 'gurning' by distorting the mouth, and the third is like a large fanged half-human half-cat.

Many counties are divided into Hundreds, believed to be an area with a hundred manor houses. They were devised by the Saxons and finally by the Normans for means of tithing. Why a given town is chosen to be the capital is not mentioned. Of the parishes here, Prittlewell and Rayleigh would seem to be the more important if the history and size of the church is considered.

If leys and ancient usage have any bearing on the matter, then Eastwood and Hawkwell have the stones. But maybe a story recorded by Philip Benton, a local 19th century historian is worth considering. He tells of a Rochford woman in around 1800 who for 18 years has a recurring dream whereby a 'treasure' was buried at a certain spot near Rochford Hall. The hall has remnants in its walls of an earlier building of the Boleyn family, being the birth place of Anne Boleyn. King Henry VIIIs royal barge often sailed into Rochford on the Roach.

The tale is mainly centred on how the woman finally persuaded the hall's owner to let her dig with the aid of a workman and with the promise that if she uncovered anything she'd be guaranteed a fair share. It is said that they dug down deep until a stone was revealed. This, the woman claimed, was the top most stone in an arch under which was the treasure. Alas, it was a lone stone and no treasure was found.

The object of this story seems to be underlining the fact that we cannot believe in all our dreams, The story seems very irrelevant in a historical context but is it saying something in disguise? It is interesting from a ley/ancient site angle. The hall is but yards from the church, and the woman uncovered a stone. Dare one hope that it was there in Neolithic times and that the tale has some truth. It is in the right place if we consider the leys, four of them pass through the hall to the church. The exact nature of this treasure is not stipulated. The word can be interpreted in different ways depending on your sense of value. If standing stones are beneficial then a stone could be considered the treasure. The reader is reminded of the treasure of the Golden Cross in Ashingdon, near Rochford, and the treasure mentioned in the ghost legend at Hadleigh.

Romford   177-513890 D. G. GM.

St. Edward's church is near the market and is a Victorian rebuild of a 15th century original. Inside are carvings in the original style. These include a pig sitting in a nest of leaves with another high up on the tower. Small squat dragons can be found, along with winged beasts with elf- like faces. On the outside of the building are green men close to two other faces that are lion like in form.

Runwell 176-754935 W.
The Running Well is the site from which the town derived its name. The well is sunk a good distance from the town in a gulley surrounded by trees just off a footpath where three fields meet, one of them rimmed with a riding track. It is about 3 feet deep and 4 x 6 feet on the surface, and fed by a small hole. It was rediscovered and researched in the early 1980s by Andrew Collins' Earth Quest group. It is thought to have received veneration by Roman times.

St. Mary's Church 176-754944 CA
Hidden beneath a drape on the inside of a door here are strange marks attributed to the devil. The legend is that a local priest called Renauldus was called in when the regular rector was taken ill. He was reputed to have dabbled in the black arts. One Sunday during a particularly fiery sermon the devil began to emerge from his mouth. Rooted to the spot in fear the congregation watched in horror as the devil rushed for the door to escape, pursued by Renauldus. But the door was closed so the creature scratched at the woodwork in a vain attempt to escape, to exit through a wall. The priest became a foul smelling pool of black liquid that seeped between the stones of the porch.

Saffron Walden 154-543385 Z.
On the east side of the common is the only surviving turf maze in Essex. It is actually a unicursal labyrinth 132 feet in diameter but if you trace the red bricks inlaid in 1978 then you will clock up about a mile. An unusual feature is the four corners that are slightly raised, half loop bastions. It was last repaired in 1699 but its age is unknown although the design goes back to 1250. Whether it is built on a geomantically derived site is another question, although I can find no leys through it. However, I have personally experienced a slight headache, as others have, on completion of its coils. I have also witnessed it have a disorientating effect on somebody, causing him to head off afterwards in the wrong direction. I personally find that the local church does this to me.

The purpose of mazes is unknown. It is probably that monks in the Middle Ages would walk them as penance. We know that this example once has an ash tree in its 33 foot centre. The ash is significant in Norse mythology as being Yggdrasil, the world tree that links three dimensions. It could thus have a symbolic meaning.

St. Mary's Church 154-538387 A. D. G. SC.

In Essex this church is second only to Thaxted in size and gargoyle population. High on the north side is a wonderful line of gargoyles and grotesques, many in animal form. Amongst the latter are a fox, and a bull laying down complete with a saddle. Also there is a hare that is crouching in a similar manner to that at Sheering church. In a corner lurks a compact crouching figure of a man holding a torch with his arms and legs in a jumble and with a large bat peering out between them! The meaning of this is elusive. If gargoyles are meant to scare evil spirits away then this one is more inclined to make them scratch their heads in bemusement or laugh!

A cat is featured, and something that looks like a phoenix, a very old rebirth symbol. We also find a wyvern and a monkey on a chain, which, oddly, is the ancient symbol for Thoth in one form; the god of literature and science, but Thoth is Egyptian. On the south side is a creature that is either another phoenix or a dove. A few nondescript animals can be seen together with a lion.

Incorporated into the wall on the east side of the tower is a stone that is the remains of the village preaching cross. Inside the building are several solar symbols in the shape of Catherine wheels.

The town itself has a number of buildings, from an antique shop to a bank that have carvings that give the overall impression that the area was once steeped in sun worship and connections with literature.

Dave Hunt is perhaps the leading researcher of the strange, clues to be found here. The pargetting (mouldings in plaster) on the one time Sun Inn tells a tale. Done in the 17th or 18th century the main feature depicts two men with clubs facing each other across a faded 12 spoke cart wheel. The full tale occupies several issues of the *ASH* magazine but I will give a fair rendering of the salient points.

One figure is a Tom Hickathrift who lived, the legend tells, near Wisbech in Cambridgeshire at the time of William the Conqueror. He was a stupid boy but a giant by the age of ten who lazed about after his father died. A farmer offered his mother two bales of straw, and Tom was persuaded to fetch them. Tom was offered as much as he could carry, but he shocked the farmer as he was able to lift a wagon load. The huge boy was not even hampered when, on the next trip, two boulders were hidden in the bale. Tom simply complained about not being given clean straw. News spread of Tom's capabilities and soon more people wanted him to work for them, including a brewer from Kings Lynn who wanted beer taken to Wisbech. Eventually Tom found that he could shorten this journey by cutting across the land of a giant who came angrily out of his cave to threaten to knock his head off! The giant mustered a huge club so Tom took off the wheel of his cart for a shield, using the axle for his weapon. Hickathrift battered the giant's head off and then found a treasure hoard in the cave. Tom went on to defeat all manner of further adversaries like highwaymen and devils.

Another version of the story has Tom challenging a wicked Baron who confiscates the villager's food and cattle. If we look at the folk tale of the Holly and Oak kings who represent the waxing and the waning sun year halves then we may note elements of this solar worship in Tom's escapades. It is interesting to also note that in Cornwall there are also stories of Tom and his ogre slaying exploits complete with cart wheels and axles. It surely must be a nation wide tale where the names of the locations are changed so that people can identify with them. For instance there are no caves within 50 miles of Wisbech.

Tom and the giant, perhaps Gog and Magog of Cambridge-shire, if symbolising summer and winter remind me of days not so long ago when the Baron/giant of winter brought hardship, cold and often starvation, it was a time most unwelcome so it was no surprise that an allegorical tale favouring the sun/Oak King/Tom has survived to this day. People were far more affected by, and aware of the seasons, a mood that lingers today in village festivals and as the basis of the 'holy days' or sabbats of the growing pagan revival today. The 12 spoke wheel on the old Sun Inn surely portrays the 12 signs of the zodiac, that rotates in the sky as does Tom's wheel on its axle.

Do the carvings and mouldings in Saffron Walden relate to this pagan interaction and dependence of the heavenly bodies, especially the sun? Let us look at other giants and characters from mythology. Ogmios was a the Celtic Lord of the Sun who wielded a club - like Hercules who is also a zodiac lord, hence his 12 labours. Ogmios is celebrated on New Year's Day in Scotland as Hogmanay; Ogma being the Irish version. He is also the inventor of the ogham alphabet; an early script of lines something like Nordic runes invented by Odin. The Greek Hermes discovered the Greek alphabet by noting the formation of flying cranes. Helios is the Greek Sun god.

So what has the town to offer? Remember the chained monkey, a symbol of Thoth who invented hieroglyphics. We have the cranes above the bank. Cranes appear on the Inn, too, birds sacred to Hermes. The mating dance of the crane is said to have been the basis for the pattern of the labyrinth. Grimsditch Wood is near the town; Grim is another name for Odin who perceived the runes when he wounded and hung himself from the Yggdrasil tree; an ash, as once grew in the maze. Hill street in the town was once named Helstrete, is this a reference to Helios? The street points to the maze and on to the village of Helions Bumpstead.

High up in the church we have Catherine wheels, she a fictitious martyre who was sentenced to death on a blazing cart wheel. We now recall the phoenix, a fire/rebirth sign, and the man holding a torch, a solar sign again.

Sheering

148

Further oddities decorate the Inn. Four shapes that resemble horse shoes or keyholes grace a wall. Dave Hunt thinks they may refer to the four bastion corners of the maze. Also there are some strange circular shapes a bit like yin yang symbols. My wife feels that they are foetal cranes curled up in their eggs. And finally, a single lone shape like a leg continues to puzzle us in this fascinating little town.

Sheering 167-496129 EW.

Wedged into a bend on the River Stort is a 4 acre earthwork backing on to Sheering Hall. I do not know its age but it has a ley running to it.

St. Mary's Church 167-509138 A. G. S. TP.

In the driveway to this 14th century church is a small stone a foot high that may be a mark stone. The building has one of the finest examples of porch carvings in Essex. On a corner is a kneeling man with long lair and a beard holding open the jaws of a lion! This theme is portrayed at Fobbing church but substituting the lion for a dragon. With tarot cards this is symbolic of strength but it is not known why it appears here. Two lurid tongue pokers appear to have folded wings and have very extended tongues. In grotesque style they have large heart shaped mouths with two eye teeth and distinctive bony fingers that are all the same length.

Above the door is a crouching, long eared beast that may be a hare, once associated with divination, perhaps conjuncting with the man and the lion, if we bear the tarot's usage in mind. Another corner shows a man bending down who looks like he is covered in hair. He is holding a leaf that is bigger than himself so he could represent some kind of little people from Celtic mythology. He may also be a tree spirit called a dryad or woodwose.

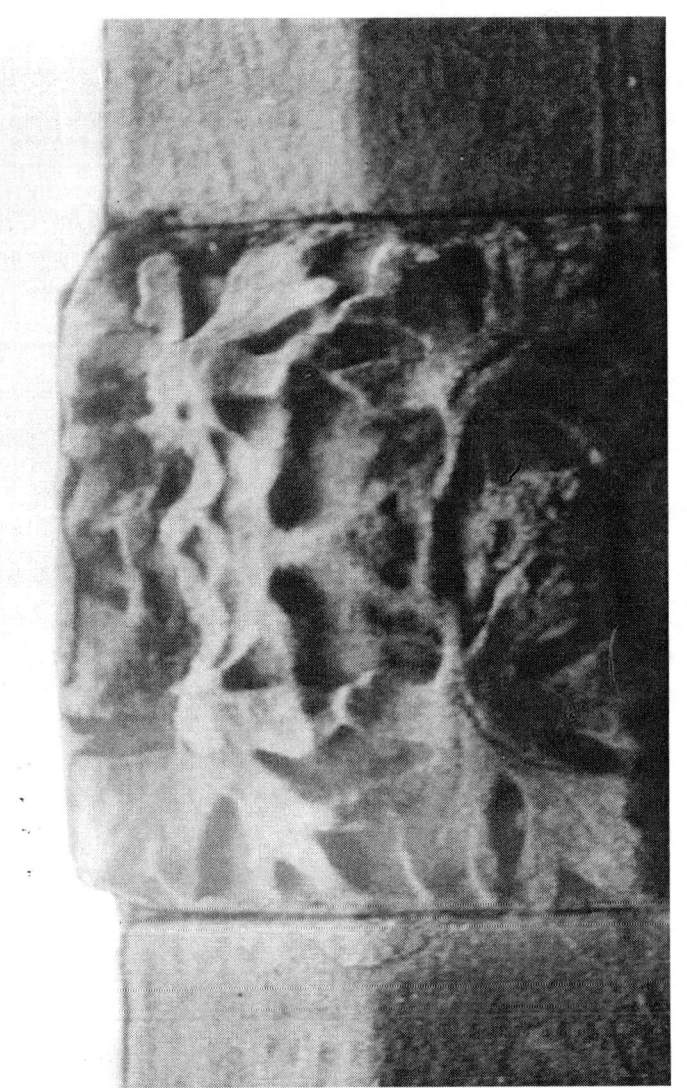

South Ockenden

Shenfield 178-605941 A. G. GM.
The old font at St. Mary's church has some flower designs with a green man, a grotesque head and an owl-like face between them.

Sible Hedingham 167-723338 S
On the main A604 road on the south edge of the village is a junction with the mill road. Flanking the drive to a large house are two rather dirty stones that may have ancient origins. The largest is 2 feet high.

St.Peter's Church 167-775344 G.
The tower has some gargoyles and inside is a medieval scratched etching on a pillar of a devil's head with a smiling face.

South Benfleet 178-779851 A.
St. Mary's church has 8 stone corbel-end carvings at roof level but more visible from a balcony. Four are pagan in origin, up in the nave corners. The are pig heads with rounded ears that tend to give the appearance of a teddy bear!

South Ockenden 177-604829 T.
Two tumuli are to be found either side of South Ockenden Hall but access is difficult as they are on private land. The north side example is marked on maps as 'The Mount'. I do not know their age but they do fall of a probable ley between Grays and Stondon Massey churches.

St. Nicholas Church 177-595829 CA. GM.
The building is mainly 13th century with Norman walls and Roman tiles included. It has a round tower and a fine Norman door with chevrons and dog tooth markings. On the same north side is an excellent green man with wide leaves blending into his whole face.

Springfield 167-730068 C.

Only discovered by aerial photography in 1987 is the cursus which helps to put Essex on the national archaeology map along side the counties of Wessex. Cursuses are the most enigmatic of all Neolithic earth workings, consisting of lone parallel banks with outer ditches that resemble narrow race courses. In size they can be up to 6 miles long and 100 yards wide. They are usually associated with round or long barrows. Only 20 or so are known. The Springfield cursus has largely been built over but was about 700 meters long with a slight kink in the middle. The ditches were not quite parallel so that it was 49 meters at the west end and 37 meters at the east end.

As usual with these structures nothing was found inside that might give any clue to its function. The few pot shards of that period were unearthed from the ditch at the eastern end where some post holes were found. These holes may have marked the foundations of later structures some of which are known to be medieval.

The ditch ends were squared off where they are usually rounded. No causeway entrances were found. A bridge may have once existed or maybe the interior was meant to go untrodden. It is doubtful that these earthworks were built to be occupied in the usual sense of the word.

Springfield Camp 167-736081 cc.

Known to be a later Saxon burial and church site and an Iron Age earthwork, this secluded site behind a supermarket and close to a footpath has only recently been discovered to be a Neolithic causeway camp. It consists of a flat central area about 50 meters across and rimmed by a low rampart and an inner ditch. Six causeways have been identified, the east/west one being the widest. Danbury church is visible on a ley line that runs in from Broomfield church. Another ley comes in from the north end and cuts along its eastern edge.

Stanford Rivers   167-534009 S.
By the road outside St. Mary's church is a stone just under 3 feet high by 2 feet across. It could be in its original position or moved from a near by cross road or the churchyard. If so it would have sat on a ley coming in from the twin churches at Willingale or from the stones at Widdington and Morton.

Stansted   167-508253 S.
Two stones guard a road junction outside the entrance to 'Garden House'. One is narrow and a yard in length while the second is similar, but fatter. Both are limestone. A possible ley runs about 300 feet from them so it would be interesting to learn if they has been moved.

St. John's Church   167-512250 A. D. G.
This 19th century building displays some fine gargoyles that were probably salvaged from the previous structure. These include two cats, one clinging sideways to a ledge and the other, a rather ugly beast with a flat nose and human like teeth, biting its own tail. Perhaps cats in high positions have little meaning other than the mason feeling that it is an obvious animal to represent. One corner has a large dogish creature similar to some at Great Waltham. It has large ears, wings and three-toed talons.

Stapleford Abbots   167-491942 EW.
Known as Lord's Walk on old O/S maps, this earthwork is now only visible in the field south of the road that cuts through it. What can be seen is a central ditch and twin ramparts that measure several hundred feet across. This section runs north to south on the land of Knoll's Hill Farm. It is not now shown on the maps but was once a ridge stretching about 1000 feet. On the 19th century maps an east-west rampart is shown north of the road. The entire structure covers around 20 acres at a guess to make it considerable larger than the sites in Epping Forest.

Stebbing

Stebbing 167-659243 EW.
On private ground in Stebbing Park is an artificial mound rising 40 feet above the surrounding moat. The flat summit is about 60 feet by 25 feet and altogether it is around 160 feet across including the moat silted on only one quarter. It is considered to be pre-Norman and not a burial mound. It is on a ley that includes the Widdington stone and Stebbing church. To visit I ventured into the grounds and was given permission by a helpful owner to wander at will. This is one of those sites that we do not expect to find in counties like Essex, it is quite a remarkable sight.

St. Mary's Church 167-664240 A. G. MP.
Here we discover a nice collection of pagan carvings including a 'devil's' head, with a beard, and a gargoyles in the shape of a monkey like creature with a large head. The mouth puller has a fairly ordinary face on a stubby body with small arms, like a squat dwarf. On the tower is a complete dog-like animal in a crouched position with its forepaws in a mouth pulling pose. Perhaps being high up was the saving grace of this animal because I can't imagine the puritans and prudists would have thrilled at its set of genitals complete with an erect phallus! This type of gargoyle alone says a lot about the real state of the Church in far off days, presenting as it does, the last kind of image that many today would associated with the religion that has become so steeped in an aversion to sex.

Stock 167-682981 T.
In a field besides the Billericay road was, or maybe still is, a barrow. It is not marked on the modern maps so maybe it has been levelled, but maps are no true indicator. I know nothing about it but it is on a ley.

All Saint's Church 167-687987 GM.
Inside, on the roof of the bell tower is an unusually coloured green man that also qualifies as a tongue poker. It also has a rim of foliage around the plaque-like flat surface it is on.

Stonebridge Hill

Stonebridge Hill 168-839291 S.
Prone on the grass verge outside Parley Beans farm by the main road is a stone that may have marked the near-by joining of three ways, or it could have been simply a plough dig. If it is a mark stone then this piece of limestone is the second heaviest I have found in Essex. At over two tons it would stand at over 4 feet and is 3 ft 6" by 2 feet in width and depth. It is on a ley that runs to Great Bromley church.

St Osyth 158-168119 D. T. W.
In the grounds of a 12th century priory a gatehouse has a carving of St. Michael and the dragon in a spandrel. There is a sacred well here on the site that once had a Temple of Isis, a popular Egyptian goddess deity of the Middle Ages. Legend has it that Osyth was a woman who lived in the early days of the Church and was beheaded by marauding Vikings for refusing to convert from her faith. At the spot sprung a well close to which the priory was built. The grounds also has a tumulus of uncertain age.

Sturmer 154-689442 T
In a field by the main road is a tumulus that manages to raise itself to a few feet in height. It is some 60 feet across and could be a worn bowl barrow or a saucer barrow. According to a guide book ancient Britons were buried here.

Sturmer Village 154-699438 S.
Beside a farm building is a rather dirty stone 2 feet across lying on its side. This specimen is good example of how a once probably important monolith can be visually relegated to an object that can be driven by and missed, as I have actually done many times before Dave Hobbs spotted it in 1993. I had a tentative 4 point ley line running down from Great Bradley church in Suffolk which I then found passed right over this stone in true 'Watkins' fashion confirming the ley line.

Terling

Sutton 178-888879 EW. LL. T.

To the north of Southend this earthwork camp is now omitted from the ordnance maps yet it covers about 8 acres. It consists of a ploughed field inside a ditch and rampart 6 feet deep and a few feet high that is covered in trees and undergrowth. It is typical of our hidden heritage as few locals are aware of its existence and no mention of it can be found in the town's museums. Yet it originally covered about 16 acres and would have 'out ranked' the camps in Epping forest.

Known as Sutton Camp and also Fosset's Camp and Grove Field, half has now vanished under the plough but the south and west sides, lost from view behind a new supermarket, are several hundred yards in length and about 40 odd feet wide. At the eastern end is a tumulus damaged by a war time gun emplacement - giving a clue to the view it commands. It is tentatively considered to be a Danish defence working, and was excavated in 1929 when Saxon pottery was found. Being as the land rises slightly to the east above the camp's level it does not really fit the defence theory. It seems more likely that it was an older converted site, if only because it entertains 3 ley lines. On my first visit in 1975 I was surprised at the view it afforded despite it being in a flat area. No less than 6 other sites were visible from its bank despite intervening urbanisation in one quarter.

Eastwood church has since been lost behind buildings but Rayleigh church, at 5.5 miles is visible with a telescope along a ley. Shopland church, now pulled down, would have been prominent, and Rochford church is visible, all being in accord with the ley energy transmission theory.

Terling 167-773149 MP. TP.

All Saint's church is chiefly 14th century with some interesting low carvings. One is a tongue poking lion. Another is a heavy man's head with forehead curls and big ears but also with clawed paws with which it holds open its mouth.

Terling

Thaxted 167-610310 A. D. G. GM. MP. TP. S.

For those into pagan decor St. John the Baptist church is the 'Mecca' of Essex churches, possessing an extravagance of stone art of every theme of the craft. With upwards of 120 carvings, the 14th century, 183 foot long cathedral-like building reflects the wealth that cutlery and wool workers brought to the town in days gone by. Its low pinnacle and corner stone gargoyles are magnificent, some as large as an Alsation dog. One such example is crouching on a buttress top in the shape of a flat faced, claw legged beast with four nobular horns. Its legs are that of a dog but its forelegs are bent up and back in a manner that no animal could be capable of. Some enthusiasts call them the 'bum scratcher' gargoyles. This distortion is a common trait with quadruped carvings; visually animal with human characteristics in the limb joints, as if a deliberate fusion - unless the mason was ignorant of the anatomy of animals.

Another beast in the same stance has a lion style mane but with a monkeyish face. On the north wall are some with more human features wearing long sleeved clothes typical of the garments of a monk, complete with raised hood. Another beast is a real grotesque creature, sitting on its haunches with semi-human arms, a mane, two stubby horns and huge cauliflower ears. In fours around the pinnacle bases are devil-like heads. One human figure has one hand pulling its mouth open.

The south wall friezes depict animals common, hybrid and fabulous. To fit into the narrow band allowed for them, as found at Sheering church and elsewhere, they are mostly shown crouching or with their heads and bodies contorted to reduce their height. Amongst the conventional we find a cat or rabbit with its paws tucked under its chin. Another is a stag with its antlered head bent round across its back.

Why this induced restriction existed is a mystery. The realism of the animals varies, as is common. The rabbit is not too exact but the stag is very precise in its facial detail. Of the fabulous creatures that we can put a name to we have a phoenix with a well defined beak and feathers. What may be a griffin appears to have wings, a long tail and a pointed head, although it may be a purely imaginative thing.

A small 'mammal' next to the cat has a tapered head with two horns. A dragon is curled in a ball and is not unlike the pair at Bowers Gifford church. One oddity might be a dragon but looks rather like a swirl of foliage with an ear poking out of it!

A tongue poker comes in the shape of a curly haired pig. A green man has leaves issuing from its hair, eyebrows and moustache in the same broad leaf fashion as at South Ockenden. Another has leaves sprouting from its head and mouth. We also have many strange little men, especially around the north porch and tower. One is playing a harp, another is squatting as he clutches a short shafted spear with a large arrow shaped head. One has a round, hooded face and is holding what could be a turnip or something, balanced on his knee! Another has a club, like Ogmios at Saffron Walden.

Inside we have to look on the transept screens and roof bosses to find an odd man/beast together with several dragons and winged faces. On a rear panel of an organ are more dragons, beasts, green men and a tongue poker. The latter can be found on the bosses as well. On the south transept screen are further faces and a dragon.

Thaxted could mark an ancient sacred site because a east-west ley line just south of the church includes an earthwork, a barrow and two standing stones. A stone once marked its passage here by the Guild Hall which has found its way a little to the east on the corner of a back street.

Tilbury Juxta Clare   167-759403   A. G. P.

Inside tiny St. Margaret's church in a lonely spot off the beaten track are several traces of medieval paintings. Grotesque heads look down from the corners and there is a winged beast in plaster that amusingly looks like a donkey with legs and wings made up of balloons like a christmas decoration.

Thundersley 178-782887 LL. S.
St. Peter's church has been rebuilt so is of no interest, but we gain a grand view from its ridge top placing, reflecting that its former nomination was to St. Michael, so prevalent with hill top churches. Close to the porch is a roundish stone with a pair of worn hollows that give it its name of the 'Bird Stone'. About 50 yards from the church, hidden in bushes besides the road is a squarish calcite stone about 2 feet high. A Saxon temple once graced the spot and the village name is derived from the teutonic god Thor verifying the pagan origins of the site.

As found elsewhere in Britain there is a legend of a tunnel running between Thundersley Manor and the church. Interestingly we find that a ley line traces exactly this supposed line, running from North Benfleet church to Hadleigh church.

Tillingham 168-993038 G.
The parish church tower has corner gargoyles of the fierce dogish type with straight forelegs as is often the style on towers. Access to the tower lends a magnificent close up view of these beautifully carved beasts.

Tilty 167-601268 D. LL. MP. S.
St. Mary's church once served the near-by Cistercian abbey that fell foul of the dissolution of 1536, the ruins visible in an adjacent field. Inside the small church is a relic of the abbey in the form of a piece of wood featuring a circle with a faded head flanked by two dragons. These are proper 'earth' dragons because their tails transmogrify into triple petalled leaves. Several more leaves sprout from their sinuous bodies and a cluster emerges from a sort of waist band.

In the grounds are two stones, one of limestone 2 foot high and the other a puddingstone oval about 28 inches by 21. The abbey is - as one might expect - reputed to be haunted. However, on one visit to the church with the ASH earth mysteries group, a terrier we had, that always rushes about like a dog in a dither, made a

Tilty

dash for the porch when some of us entered. The dog reached the door and skidded to a halt, took one look inside, turned and bolted for it! Only after a third attempt and with much prompting, did we finally manage to get her inside. Carole Young then informed us that the church was haunted by a monk! It seemed to have wandered over from the abbey.

Maybe reports in the *Essex Countryside* magazine that during 1976 people claimed to have seen what was described as dwarves and goblins in the area was true? There are also legends of hidden tunnels that are never found. This usually indicated a ley line, although as yet I have not found any here save a probable one from the abbey to the Henham stones.

Threshers Bush 167- 499093 LL. S.

At crossroads amidst a tiny rural scattering of houses a small reddish stone is embedded in the earth bank. This insignificant looking boulder, however, is mentioned by the old Essex Field Club. It aligns with the buttress stone at Epping Upland church and Latton Priory and Great Canfield's earthwork. The four roads feeding the cross over are all dead straight as they approach, and each one points directly to a church or a stone including one along a ley to Abbess Roding church.

A few hundred yards along the Magdelen Laver road is a puddingstone about a foot high under the corner of a barn. This may be a mark stone because it and the crossroad stone align to Latton church.

Tiptree 168-407175 EW.

Shown on the map as 'The Rampart' this site consists of simply a four foot high bank and a shallow water filled ditch. One end juts into Pods Wood and the main body stretches about half a kilometre across fields. It is not listed as being Roman. If it is the remains of an enclosure then it could have been as large as Wallbury. It is edged by three ley lines.

Twinstead 155-861367 S.
At either side of a road by the parish church are two stones. The larger is mentioned by Rudge, this being 5 feet long. He does not mention, however, a small calcite block just under a yard across. This may be a plough find that was deemed should join the other.

Ugley Green 167-524271 S.
Besides the village green, which is not the least bit ugly, - the word derived from a Saxon word - we find a well pump and a puddingstone measuring 3 ft x 4 ft x 2 ft, marking the point where three ways meet.

Dellows Lane 167-523269 S.
One of the above lanes takes a right turn a short way from the green. Wedged into the grassy bank is a lump of limestone of conical shape about 2 feet across.

Upminster 177-559867 D.
St. Lawrence's church has a 2 foot high coloured statue inside of St. George slaying a dragon.

Wakes Colne Green 168-897301 S.
On the grass verge where three ways meet in this scattered rural village lies three stones. They may well be plough finds but they align to the stones at Stonebridge Hill and Great Bardfield church. Two are by a farm entrance alongside and the other is of limestone and lays on its own across the junction triangle. It is 3 feet high and the same across and shows signs of weathering.

Waltham 166-381007 CA. D. G. GM. P. TP.
The great aisle pillars of the abbey church are adorned with Norman spirals and zig-zags. The huge ceiling features a painting of diamond shaped depictions of the signs of the zodiac, the elements of earth, air, fire and water, and the labours of

Hercules. Inside can be found tongue pokers and grotesques. In the porch are two winged dog-like grotesques, and, on pillars, an owl behind a screen of leaves, a hawk and a green man. On the pillar capitols of the south door are two dragons with foliage issuing from them.

Marsh Hill 166-394040 S.
A few miles north of Waltham at the three way meet on the B194 road is the Coach and Horses pub. Leaning against a wall is a stone of around 3 feet by 2 feet. The pub proprietor does not know when is was put there, and it was not logged by Rudge who searched that area. It is possible that it was one he found that has been moved since. Typical here, were the remarks of the landlord to Dave Hobbs and I on noticing our interest. His wife was an historian yet they had no idea of the possible significance and age of the stone, literally, on their own door step.

Holyfield 166-387030 S.
This is one of 'Rudge's' stones listed in the 1940s that has survived. It has been moved but not far enough to effect the grid reference. It is a puddingstone just over 3 feet high and now rests upright by a rough track on the south side of the road.

Wendens Ambo 151-521341 G. GM. S.
St.Mary's church has some gargoyles on an internal arch with a green man. In the drive is a small stone of knee height.

West Bergholt 168-965290 EW.
Pitchbury Ramparts is a bank and 10 foot ditch in some woods near the village extending in a curve for about 400 feet. Although near to Roman Colchester they are considered to be older. About 100 feet of it is definable, and if we follow the line of the curve it suggests that the site could have covered 8 to 10 acres.

West Hanningfield 167-735998 GM.
SS Mary and Edward church has a green man on a beam boss and three on the font. The central head has vines from its mouth that spread out and surround the other two.

Wethersfield 167-712313 S.
St. Mary Magdelen church has parts of the nave walls that may be Saxon. Testimony to the age of the site could lie with the sarsen stone that now sits by a door step neat the churchyard gate. It is fairly circular, 2 feet across by 6 inches high, and last used for horse mounting.

White Notley 167-788178 LL. S.
Mentioned by Rudge as one of the puddingstones that trail across several counties. It is 36 inches high and stands by a cottage on the roadside near Whiteways Farm. Before I found this stone I had a tentative ley line running up to Fairstead church. On extending it I found that it took in the stone.

White Roding 167-562134 G.
Carved on a corbel end at St. Martin's church is a human head with rams horns, each of which he is holding with crossed arms. This could represent Cernunnos, the Celtic horned god, Lord of the Beasts. Another figure has his left foot up against his chest in a manner similar to one at Matching church. He is the lame King of summer who was ritualistically slain by the winter Oak King of the winter solstice.

Wickham Bishops 168-825113 LL.
The church of this village is 19th century and built on a new site close to the centre. The old medieval church fell into disuse but it is currently being restored, though too small for a congregation. It is a delightful little building restored to the O/S map after a long absence. It lays close to the River Blackwater and is one of those churches where the villagers had a long walk to attend the

services. A ley line hits it up from Blackwall Bridge. Another may run to Beeleigh Tumulus.

This area is a maze of criss-crossing roads and is well wooded. 900 years ago in the year 1000 AD it would have been very heavily forested. Legend has it that a green man dwelt in the woods at near-by Little Braxted. Even by then much felling had taken place, so much so that the little man was the last survivor of many in the area. Nearly 1000 years old he was worried that if he reached this significant age the devil would capture his soul. In his plight he sought the help of the local bishop - from whom the town may have been named - who arranged a game of chess with the devil to take place on the day before the green man's birthday, the 21st of June, Midsummers Day. The venue was on an old oak tree stump where two sheep tracks met at Wickham.

That night the green man slept where 3 sheep tracks met at Little Braxted. The bishop slept where 4 tracks met at Wickham at the opposite side to the old stump because the devil would not sit the next day where the Bishop slept.

Next morning, the game lasted all day until the bishop was finally victorious. The deal was adhered to and the green man was assured his place in heaven. As the years passed a pub was built on the site of the stump called the Chequers. Where the green man slept eventually rose another pub called the Green Man. In Wickham, where the bishop slept the subsequent pub is called the Mitre.

From this tale we can extract elements of pagan solar worship. Note the date; the summer solstice. The bishop may correspond to the Holly King - some say that the word holy is derived from holly - and the devil is the Oak King. The bishop/Holly King rules over the sunniest half of the year and the devil/Oak King the dreaded grip of winter.

But in defeating the devil the bishop ensures that the fructifying energy of spring would bring forth greenery, food and warmth. The green man would be here, in other words, and not be in the

Willingale Doe

custody of the devil winter as he would if having lost his soul to him.

The thousand years that the green man was fearful of reaching may stem from the biblical tale of Satan being cast down for 1000 years, the number thus becoming symbolic of the devil. Is it coincidence that the Green Man pub in its picturesque setting is on a ley line from Witham to Little Totham churches?

Wickham St. Paul 155-816367 S.
On the grass at a cross road near Mount Farm not far from Gestingthorpe lies a large block of limestone similar in form to one at Ovington with its bubbled appearance. It is 4 feet high by 3 feet across.

Widdington 167-533322 S.
To the north of the village where three roads meet is a large puddingstone, measuring 4 feet by 3 feet, on a tiny central overgrown triangular island. This stone is the only one I have found in Essex that has the qualities of Watkin's aligned mark stones. One face has been sheered flat as if a direction indicator. On projecting the angle on a map I find that it points directly to the tumulus in Quendon Park one way and to Debden church the other. Further searching may show this to be a ley line, as yet it has only 4 points.

Willingale 167-596073 G. LL. S.
Two churches oddly share the same churchyard here representing the parishes of Willingale Doe and Willingale Spain, their names stemming from Norman land owners. Why the duality is a subject for speculation, the popular belief is that the said Normans were rivals and so would not set foot in a church built by the other. Another legend is that the two protagonists were feuding sisters. These tales as such are not viable because the two buildings were erected 200 years apart in time, 'Spain' the smaller and possible of Saxon origins.

It may have some bearing on the latter legend to mention a large house in Wensleydale, Yorkshire where for an unknown reason in the 18th century the centre section of the house was removed and not rebuilt. One tale is that is was to exorcise a ghost, the other that it was the result of a feud between two sisters, so one house became two so that they could avoid talking to each other. Could this coincidence be an example of a common theme? Could sisters be equated with goddesses or female energy?

Furthermore, the idea of twin churches seems odd for another reason. If we had two parishes then, as elsewhere, we would expect two sites, especially if there was a feud. We might then expect the churches to be as far apart as possible, maybe, not next door to one another.

Thinking geomantically, 1 am tempted to wonder if the ground beneath the site was particularly rich in ch'i energy so as to be considered to have been too good to resist by both parishes. Maybe two stones stood here on this ridge spot with a commanding view.

The larger of the two, 'Doe' has a tower which displays a gargoyle's head with wide flat fins issuing from its cheeks. They are somewhat leaf-like and could be intended to be a green man.

Just to the south of the churches where three ways meet is a stone wedged into a grassy bank. It is barely 18 inches across but plays host to two of the five leys I have found running here. One comes in from Fyfield church and goes on to Blackwall Bridge. Another starts at the stone and skims the churchyard to continue to a stone in Great Dunmow.

Witham 168-825153 EW.
Now completely cut in two by the railway it is difficult to assess the size of this earthwork. It is recorded in the Saxon chronicle that in 913 AD Edward the Elder founded it. But it is considered that it may have been simply altered as were so many others.

St. Nicholas' Church 168-818153 A. G. MP. TP.
The tower here has a number of carvings including lions that are both tongue poking and mouth pulling. For some reason lions seem to be the favourite animal for such facial distortions. In mythology and religion the lion would not figure in Celtic or European pagan pantheons, not being an indigenous beast. It would be known in Christendom because it inhabited the Near East and Palestine up to the Middle Ages. Of course the Romans used them in their amphitheatres. A winged lion is the Lion of Judah and the Church used it to represent the kingly power of Christ and also for the devil who is a roaring lion with intent of devouring people. St. Mark, one of the four evangelists is carved as a lion on churches and it co-responds to fire, solar power and is associated with various sun gods. To many cultures it is the king of beasts, and a noble and revered animal, so why we have them tongue poking is an open question.

Witham church is on a pagan site and the town was founded by the enigmatic Knights Templar.

Wormingford 168-932323 CA. D.
Although St. Andrew's church was intensively restored in Victorian times it has a stained glass window that tells of dragons. The lower of two of these beasts is actually a crocodile. The story is that one was bought back from Egypt by the crusaders in the reign of Richard the Lionheart. It was kept at the Tower of London and grew and grew until it finally escaped into the Thames. It eventually made its way up the River Stour crawling ashore at Wormingford. Legend has it that the fearful villagers fed it on virgins until they ran out - or ran away I would imagine - so a knight was summoned to despatch it. This was duly done in what is now called Bloody Meadow. The green crocodile in the stained glass is shown in the act of gobbling a virgin!

The notion that dragons enjoy the taste of virgins may have fertility overtones. They are also the accomplice of St. George and St. Michael, the former usually rescuing a maiden/virgin from its fatal clutches. The villagers try to keep the beast alive at first, as if revered, enough so anyway to sacrifice their young ladies to it. Why didn't they call in the dragon-buster right away? The saints are portrayed as sometimes restraining the dragon on a leash whilst ready with a weapon in the other hand. It is as if the beast represents something worth much sacrifice as long as it does not get out of hand, nothing is said - assuming the legend has any sense - of the knight not being immediately available or waiting in the wings, so to speak, so if not fed the dragon becomes dangerous.

St. George and St.Michael are featured in the window, the latter holding his usual flaming sword but has the red dragon on a lead, backing this theory that saints are meant to be harnessing the creature. Michael is poised ready to put his sword in.

In one hand the saint is also holding a pair of scales with the bible in one cup and a tiny dragon in the other symbolising the triumph of Christianity over paganism, the bible shown weighing the most.

A second legend of that era gave the village its name. Worm or orm are terms tied in with dragons and serpents. In around the 17th century a huge dragon is said to have appeared on the estates of Sir Richard Waldergrave on the Suffolk side of the river near Bures. It was attacked but could not be defeated until eventually it disappeared into a lake and was never seen again. An odd story this, with no romantic overtones or ending.

The central pillars of the church are covered in centuries old graffiti scratched on them, including initials and an odd symbol that might be a family crest. Also is a Vesica Pisces (vessel of the fish) on two pillars that are not roughly etched but must have been drawn with an instrument. These overlapping circles are the basis of sacred geometry, a root design from which all else geometric can be derived. It could be that the church builders used the pattern, as was common, as a base for the ground layout. Much of what is known as sacred, Golden Mean geometry and the science of numbers and form was later banned so that we today do not learn this fascinating aspect of nature's building blocks in schools any more.

Bibliography

ASH (Albion's Sacred Heritage) magazine. Editors Ian Dawson and Dave Hunt. £1.75p a copy quarterly. Subscription for 4 @ £6.50p. Info; from 2 Kent View Road, Vange, Basildon, Essex SS16 4LA.

The Aquarian Guide to British and Irish Mythology. John and Caitlin Matthews, Aquarian Press, 1988.

The British Maze Guide, Adrian Fisher and Jeff Saward. Minotaur designs, 1991.

At The Edge magazine. 2 Cross Hill Close, Wymeswold, Loughborough, Leicestershire, LE12 6UJ.

Caerdroia. Annual magazine of so named maze and labyrinth research group. Details from 53 Thundersley Grove, Thundersley, Essex SS7 3EB.

Discovering Churchyards. Mark Child. Shire Publications, 1982.

Dragons, their history and symbolism, Janet Hoult. Gothic Image Publications, 1987.

Essex Naturalist Magazine. Articles by Dr E. A. Rudge, circa 1949-52, Stored at main Essex libraries.

Feng Shui, The Elements of. Joanne O Brien and Kwok Nam Ho. Element Books, 1991.

The Kings England, Essex. Arthor Mee. Hodder and Stoughton, 1966.

London Earth Mysteries Circle. Journal. Details from; LEMC P.O Box 1035 London WC2 6ZX.

Needles of Stone. Tom Graves. Turnhouse Books, 1978.

The Old Straight Track. Alfred Watkins. Abacus, 1974.

Standing Stones and Mark Stones, of Leicestershire and Rutland. Bob Trubshaw. Heart of Albion Press, 1991.

Essex ley line map

A five colour map is available of Essex, that includes around 70 ley lines of five points and above, derived using Watkin's criteria, and is the result of 20 years of years to research.

The scale is 4.5mm to 1 km or 1 inch to 4 miles approx. It measures 17" x 20".

The map has 11 types of symbol depicting all the sites mentioned in this book, including those not on ley lines. Graphically it includes Roman roads, woods, towns and rivers in colour shading.

The border surround is decorated with artwork drawings of gargoyles taken from photographs of the Great Waltham devil, Great Bromley man-eating dragons, Tilty dragons, Ardleigh beast, South Ockenden green man, Arkesden wyvern and a Kelveden dog-gargoyle.

Over 45 sites in surrounding Kent, Herts, Cambs, and Suffolk are included.

Price is £5.00p including p&p, from 4 Tiptree Close, Leigh on Sea, Essex. SS9 4BA.

Index

Abbey, 61, 67, 117, 127, 135, 142, 163, 165-166
Ambresbury Banks, 14, 86, 89, 127, 135
Astrology, 10, 44, 85
Avebury, 3, 6, 12, 16, 49, 52, 96

Barrow, 19-20, 63, 71, 80, 114, 127, 155, 157, 162
Beacon Hill, 17, 58, 67, 135
Beeleigh Abbey, 127, 135, 142
Beeleigh Tumulus, 67, 169
Benton, Phili, 112, 142
Bird Stone, 27, 163
Bowles farm, 142
Bushes Farm, 117

Castle, 5, 15-16, 22, 28, 41, 48, 56, 58, 68, 77, 81, 83, 105, 107, 112-113, 140-141
Causeway Camp, 13, 15-16, 61, 152
Celts, 11, 23, 31
Ceridwen, 43, 71
Cernunnos, 168

Ch'i, 10-11, 15-17, 20-21, 39, 102, 111, 172
China, 9, 17, 41
Cranes, 147, 149
Cursus, 48, 61, 72, 127, 152

Danes, 5, 96
Dene Hole, 61
Devil, 33, 39, 53, 68-69, 71, 76, 86, 91, 102, 112, 115, 117, 144, 151, 155, 169, 171, 173, 178
Downham church, 124
Dowsing, 11, 35, 53
Dragon project, 11
Dragon, 9-11, 39, 41, 53, 56, 61, 65, 69, 72-73, 85, 87, 93-95, 97, 102, 114-115, 123-124, 140, 149, 157, 162, 166, 174
Dryad, 149

Earthwork, 6, 15, 55-56, 58, 61, 67, 77, 81, 86, 89, 95, 103, 115, 124-125, 135, 137-138, 140-141, 149, 152-153, 159, 162, 165, 172
Easthorpe church, 58, 83, 95
Egyptian, 21, 43, 126, 145, 157
Essex field Club, 2, 56, 59, 127, 165
Exhibitionist, 61

Feng Shui, 9-10, 15, 17, 21, 27, 102, 121, 138, 176
Foliage, 36, 43, 65, 75, 95, 99, 102, 112, 134, 139, 155, 162, 167

179

Folk-lore, 21, 26, 36, 45, 53, 99
Font, 61, 63, 73, 75, 87, 126, 151, 168
Fortification Wood, 135
Fosset's Camp, 159
Fylfot, 126

Gargoyle, 2, 33, 36-37, 87, 119, 123, 145, 155, 172
Gentry's Farm, 55, 75
Geomancer, 10, 53
Glastonbury Tor, 7, 22
Golden Cross, 55, 66-67, 143
Goldens Farm, 66
Goldsticks Farm, 66, 68, 81
Green man, 36-37, 56, 61, 72, 75, 87, 91, 99, 102-103, 115, 125, 129, 133-134, 151, 155, 162, 167-169, 171-172, 178
Greenbank House, 105
Griffin, 2, 33, 43, 161
Grotesque, 36-37, 55, 77, 81, 83, 97, 115, 142, 149, 151, 161-162
Grove, 61, 68, 75, 134, 159, 176

Hangman's Wood, 95
Hatfield Forest, 71
Henge, 15-16, 49, 61, 63
Herne, 37, 118
High Woods, 130
Hill Fort, 15, 48
Hobbs Hole, 137
Holly King, 130, 169
Holy Hill, 61, 71
Holy Well (see Well)

Jumping Stone, 103

King Cnut, 32, 51, 67, 76
Knights Templar, 51, 89, 173

Labyrinth, 21-22, 144, 147, 176
Leper Stone, 58, 124, 135-136
Ley lines, 1, 20, 45, 47, 51, 57, 61, 77, 94, 127, 133, 137-138, 142, 159, 165, 178
Limestone, 8, 11, 73, 75, 79, 105, 112, 114, 123, 127, 129, 137, 153, 157, 163, 166, 171
Lord's Walk, 58, 153
Lucus Farm, 58, 68, 79, 135

Maze, 21-22, 61, 126, 144, 147, 149, 169, 176
Melbourne, Derbyshire, 87
Moore's Ditch, 94
Mount Farm, 171
Mouth Puller, 61, 155

Norsey Woods, 71
Nwyvre, 11, 20

Oak King, 130, 147, 168-169
Odin, 99, 102, 147
Othona, 73

Painting, 61, 109, 166
Parley Beans Farm, 157
Phoenix, 33, 43, 145, 147, 161
Pickingill, George, 77
Pinchpools House, 127
Pitchbury Ramparts, 167
Plumberow Mount, 18, 56, 58, 117

Porch, 28-29, 56, 65, 69, 72, 76, 83, 86, 93, 95, 99, 115, 121, 124, 129, 140, 144, 149, 162-163, 165, 167
Portingbury Hills, 71
Preaching Cross, 50, 55-56, 61, 67, 75, 79, 117, 124, 142, 145
Puddingstone, 26, 65-66, 117, 119, 127, 129, 131, 133, 163, 165-167, 171

Roman, 20-21, 23, 25, 27, 32, 36, 50, 73, 83, 85, 89-90, 93, 96, 99, 114, 117, 123, 126, 129-130, 140, 144, 151, 165, 167, 178
Rood screen, 65, 91, 115

Sarsen stone, 8, 73, 79, 119, 168
Saxons, 5-6, 19, 73, 141-142
Scots Pine, 50, 56, 121, 134
Sheela-na-gig, 35, 41, 83
Shopland church, 139, 159
Silbury Hill, 13, 19, 96
Solar carving, 61
St. Catherine, 99
St. George, 39, 85, 87, 97, 114, 140, 166, 173-174
St. Lawrence, 55-56, 58, 66, 72, 87, 89, 111, 166
St. Margaret, 39, 65, 72, 129, 162
St. Michael, 17, 39, 67, 73, 85, 93, 109, 123, 137-138, 140, 157, 163, 173-174
St.Augustine, 32
Standing stone, 20, 51, 103, 135, 138

Standon, Herts, 26
Statues, 37, 65
Stone circle, 52-53, 63, 121
Stonehenge, 3, 8, 16, 25, 49
Sun Inn, 146-147
Swastika, 99

Tarot, 93, 149
Tongue Poker, 37, 61, 72-73, 79, 81, 85, 97, 109, 113, 142, 155, 162
Tumulus, 49, 56, 58, 61, 67, 71, 89, 117, 123, 130, 135, 138, 157, 159, 169, 171

Venus Stone, 55, 67, 80, 114, 141

Wallbury Camp, 57-58, 125, 138-139
Wares Farm, 129
Witch, 43, 91, 105, 107, 125-126
Witches Stone, 105
Woden (see Odin)
Woodwose, 149
Wyvern, 41, 65, 93, 97, 125, 145, 178

Yew tree, 97, 129
Yin & Yang, 10, 15, 21, 27, 39, 121, 149

Zodiac, 44, 85, 147, 166

FREE DETAILED CATALOGUE

A detailed illustrated catalogue is available on request, SAE or International Postal Coupon appreciated. Titles are available direct from Capall Bann, post free in the UK (cheque or PO with order) or from good bookshops and specialist outlets. Title currently available include:

Animals, Mind Body Spirit & Folklore
Angels and Goddesses - Celtic Christianity & Paganism by Michael Howard
Arthur - The Legend Unveiled by C Johnson & E Lung
Auguries and Omens - The Magical Lore of Birds by Yvonne Aburrow
Book of the Veil The by Peter Paddon
Call of the Horned Piper by Nigel Jackson
Cats' Company by Ann Walker
Celtic Lore & Druidic Ritual by Rhiannon Ryall
Compleat Vampyre - The Vampyre Shaman: Werewolves & Witchery by Nigel Jackson
Crystal Clear - A Guide to Quartz Crystal by Jennifer Dent
Earth Dance - A Year of Pagan Rituals by Jan Brodie

Earth Magic by Margaret McArthur
Enchanted Forest - The Magical Lore of Trees by Yvonne Aburrow
Healing Homes by Jennifer Dent
Herbcraft - Shamanic & Ritual Use of Herbs by Susan Lavender & Anna Franklin
In Search of Herne the Hunter by Eric Fitch
Inner Space Workbook - Developing Counselling & Magical Skills Through the Tarot
Kecks, Keddles & Kesh by Michael Bayley
Living Tarot by Ann Walker
Magical Incenses and Perfumes by Jan Brodie
Magical Lore of Animals by Yvonne Aburrow
Magical Lore of Cats by Marion Davies

Magical Lore of Herbs by Marion Davies
Masks of Misrule - The Horned God & His Cult in Europe by Nigel Jackson
Mysteries of the Runes by Michael Howard
Oracle of Geomancy by Nigel Pennick
Patchwork of Magic by Julia Day
Pathworking - A Practical Book of Guided Meditations by Pete Jennings
Pickingill Papers - The Origins of Gardnerian Wicca by Michael Howard
Psychic Animals by Dennis Bardens
Psychic Self Defence - Real Solutions by Jan Brodie
Runic Astrology by Nigel Pennick
Sacred Grove - The Mysteries of the Forest by Yvonne Aburrow
Sacred Geometry by Nigel Pennick
Sacred Lore of Horses The by Marion Davies
Sacred Ring - Pagan Origins British Folk Festivals & Customs by Michael Howard
Secret Places of the Goddess by Philip Heselton
Talking to the Earth by Gordon Maclellan
Taming the Wolf - Full Moon Meditations by Steve Hounsome
The Goddess Year by Nigel Pennick & Helen Field
West Country Wicca by Rhiannon Ryall
Witches of Oz The by Matthew & Julia Phillips

Capall Bann is owned and run by people actively involved in many of the areas in which we publish. Our list is expanding rapidly so do contact us for details on the latest releases. We guarantee our mailing list will never be released to other companies or organisations.

Capall Bann Publishing, Freshfields, Chieveley, Berks, RG20 8TF.